ALL THAT...
THE OTHER HALF OF HISTORY

To Jane, Happy birthday
Happy reading! Love Hilary.

■ After having been born in Barnsley, **Kate Charlesworth** went to art college in Manchester and hung about there longer than necessary. She now lives in London, working as a freelance illustrator and cartoonist (work always welcome). She does not have a cat.

Scottish born and bred, **Marsaili Cameron** staggered south to find fame and/or fortune but continued to be a writer and editor instead. After an educational time working at the Open University, she flung caution to the wind and went freelance in London. She has never drawn a cartoon (or straight line) in her life.

ALL THAT...
THE OTHER HALF OF HISTORY

Kate Charlesworth
and Marsaili Cameron

PANDORA

First published in 1986
by Pandora Press
(Routledge & Kegan Paul Ltd)
11 New Fetter Lane, London EC4P 4EE

Published in the USA by
Routledge & Kegan Paul Inc.
in association with Methuen Inc.
29 West 35th Street, New York, NY 10001

Set in Plantin and Univers
and printed in Great Britain
by Butler & Tanner Ltd
Frome and London

Library of Congress Cataloging in Publication Data

Charlesworth, Kate.
All that

Bibliography: p.
1. Great Britain——History, Comic, satirical, etc.
2. Women——Great Britain——Anedotes, facetiae, satire,
etc. I. Cameron, Marsaili. II. Title.
DA33.C47 1986 941'.0088042 86–13895

British Library CIP Data also available

ISBN 0-86358-067-X

To Vanessa Nias from Kate Charlesworth

To Marjorie and Jack Cameron and to Sonja Ruehl from Marsaili Cameron.

Elizabeth Blackadder · Margaret Harrisson
Artists
Barbara Jones · Jessie King · Enid Marx · Julia Margaret Cameron
Joan Hassal · Gertrude Hermes · Gwen Raverat · Clarice Cliff
Mary Beale 1632-1697 Painter
Gluck (H. Gluckstein) b. 1895 Painter
May Morris. Designer 1862-1938 Jeweller Embroiderer
Dame Laura Knight. 1877-1970. Painter
Dame Barbara Hepworth. 1903-1975 Sculptor
Eileen Grey Designer. 1879-1976
Gwen John 1876-1939 painter
Bridget Riley Painter b. 1931
Elizabeth Montgomerey b. 1902
Sophia Harris 1901-66
Peggy Harris b. 1904
'MOTLEY' Stage design group
Angelica Kauffman. 1741-1807. Painter
(Dorothy) Brett Painter & Eccentric 1883-1978
(Dora) Carrington 1893-1932 Painter
Susie Cooper b. 1902. Ceramic designer
Vanessa Bell. Painter. 1879-1961
Margaret Macdonald Designer. Metalworker Stained Glass 1865-1933
'Observer' Jane Bown Photographer from 1950
Marion Dorn 1899-1964 Carpet & textile design
Kate Greenaway 1846-1901 Illustrator
The Durham Quilters
Julia Trevelyan Oman. Stage designer
Elizabeth Frink b. 1930 Sculptor
Katherine Pleydell-Bouverie Potter
Mabel-Lucie Atwell. Illustrator
Lady Butler Eliz. c. 1844-1933. Painter
Beryl Cook. Painter
Beatrix Potter 1866-1943 Illustrator
(Cartoonists) - (Anton · Margo Belsky · Posy Simmonds

Contents

Contents

Preface

Research during the last fifteen years or so has resulted in a major new discovery. It now appears clear that, contrary to all assumptions, *there were women in English History*. The implications of this finding defy description (so, relax). But the fact remains that those refusing to acknowledge this blow to the status quo are likely to experience grave difficulty in holding conversations with their mothers and daughters, avoiding street interviews, getting the right change for the launderette, etc.

With this worrying situation in mind, we have devised an interactive learning programme which will enable you to update and expand your historical knowledge. The need is all the more pressing since we understand that, in removing most textbooks from most classrooms across the land, our government may have eliminated the only extant text to have brought history within most people's grasp. We refer, of course, to Sellar and Yeatman's classic *1066 and All That*.

However, although the overall authority of this work is undisputed, the date of its first publication – 1930 – meant that the authors couldn't be aware that women existed in any numbers throughout history. For this reason, we have thought it appropriate, while building on their memorable foundations, to bring the historical record up to date.

Due to educational deprivation or allergy to serious study, some of you may be unfamiliar with Sellar and Yeatman's standard work. *Nil desperandum* (trans. 'Dinna' fash yoursel'). Our book, devised along the most progressive educational lines, is entirely self-standing (though we wouldn't advise you to prop anything else up with it). The only essential prerequisite for would-be learners is prior attendance at school until the age of ten.

Some of you may already be acquainted with research in the area of women and history; in which case you're likely to be bubbling over with curiosity as to the *criteria for selection* which we have used in compiling our material. The answer, we like to think, is elegantly simple: the main criterion, applied rigorously by both of us, is *personal idiosyncrasy*. That is, we've put in the events, people and trends that we'd heard of and that appealed to us and we've left out the rest.

Pursuing this streamlined course, we have attempted to keep original research down to a minimum, relying wherever possible on second, third and fourth hand versions of events. Sadly, though, this objective could not always be achieved and at times you will read and see things here which cannot be found anywhere else.

We would point out, however, that the less inclined you are to believe some of the information contained in the text, the more likely it is to be true. Where they do occur, our embellishments are but pale shadows of the peculiar world in which women have lived for so long. We do include the odd queen (in fact, one or two very odd queens indeed) but on the whole we have concentrated on the rough trade of history. Well, it's nice to feel at home, isn't it?

KC
MC

Acknowledgments

We made up some of the material in this book, but an astonishing amount of it is true. Our first debt of gratitude therefore is due to the women across the centuries who are quoted here; and to the authors and editors cited in our sources who made many of these voices accessible to twentieth-century readers.

Our second debt of overwhelming gratitude is due to our researcher, Judith Harrad, who gave up week-day lunches for five months in order to scour libraries for information which could begin to fill the black holes of our ignorance. We hope that some of her discoveries – like the existence of a nineteenth-century organisation called The National Truss Society for the Relief of the Ruptured Poor – went some way to compensate her; but who knows better than she the truth of the saying, 'There's no such thing as a free lunch-time'?

We would like to thank Virago for letting us see photographs of the following authors: M. J. Farrell (Molly Keane); Enid Bagnold; Rose Macaulay; Harriet Martineau; Sybille Bedford; May Sinclair; Elizabeth Taylor; and Dorothy Richardson.

Chatto & Windus kindly lent us a photograph of Sylvia Townsend Warner.

Many friends gave us support and encouragement in our bizarre project, in some cases enduring with remarkable patience the gruesome spectacle of two adult human beings laughing at their own jokes. Special thanks to Sibyl Grundberg, Gillian Hanscombe, Alison Hennegan, Julia Johnson, Andrew Lumsden of *The New Statesman,* Vanessa Nias, Marney Queen, Beryl Ruehl, Sonja Ruehl, Prunella Sedgwick, Annie Sidford, Gail Vines, Jeffrey Weeks.

MODULE 1

Pre-history or *Before video-recorded time*

Why it's called 'pre-history', we can't imagine. Just like the Real Thing, it's used to instruct us all on everyday twentieth-century living.

You know the kind of thing. After having gone through the Ape Phase (embarrassing in retrospect but he *was* young and foolish), Man the Hunter stood up straight and had his first thought. He instantly proceeded to tuck up Wee Wifie and brood in a cave, donned his hunting pink and was off to pursue his chosen vocation. On his sweating return, he kindly spread round some of the bounty (secured by means of his terrific new spear) before settling down to work on a serious mural or two. Still full of primitive vim and vigour, he later took masterful advantage of the secondary (not to mention primary) sex characteristics which Wee Wifie had obligingly sprouted to keep him home and happy.

That's how we're programmed today, the story goes, so we defy our inheritance at our peril.

Laugh – we could have died. Pull the other ancient artefact, do.

ACTIVITY

Project yourself back into a Golden Age where you've never heard of Desmond Morris, Robert Ardrey, Lionel Tiger or any other defender of the male faith in aggression. Then make up your own diary entry for Great-great-great-to-the-power-of-x Grandmama. You may want to cast caution to the winds and include such esoteric activities as:

- developing grinding stones
- gathering seeds, nuts, berries, leaves and grubs
- thinking up the idea of pottery

Having fooled around with the subversive idea that Great-great-etc. Grandmama was not a complete dumbo (or at least not more of a dumbo than Great-great-etc. Granddad), you may want to indulge in a little further light scepticism. Does your body indeed look the way it does today because it evolved to put a gleam in a pre-historic male eye?

At least one writer is bloody sure it didn't. In her book, *The Descent of Woman*, Elaine Morgan argues that the female secondary sex characteristics (in particular, head hair, breasts and buttocks) evolved to make life easier for the nipper's nippers rather than the nipper himself. If you see what we mean. In the semi-aquatic life which she visualises for our ancestors, Elaine Morgan suggests that the baby anthropoid had such great and pressing need for things to hang on to that luxuriant head hair and pronounced breasts were eventually granted to mama. The larger female buttocks developed partly to provide protection for the woman while sitting breast-feeding on a pebbly beach. (Yes, you may well wince.)

A pretty bizarre notion? Well, frankly, all explanations of why we look the way we do now have something of the call of the cuckoo about them. But, there you are – or, rather, here *we* are, an odd-looking race altogether. So do feel quite free to think up your own implausible theories for our implausible appearance.

And now on to the difficult matter of Ages. Do you remember Mrs Disraeli speaking for all of us in the nineteenth century when she remarked that she could never remember which came first, the Greeks or the Romans? Well, forget about the Greeks and the Romans – they come later (and in that order); but admit, do, to a certain wobbliness with regard to the sequence of the pre-historic Ages. One's on safe ground, of course – and can indeed sound authoratitive – when dealing with the Old, Middle and New Stone Ages. Only if assailed by a sudden worry that BC times require a reversal of adjectives as well as figures would one hesitate to claim that the New Stone Age showed many advances on the Old.

Self-check question

Which came first, the New Stone Age or the Old?

You're a smart lot – thought we'd got you bamboozled there.

However, it's a different matter when it comes to other materials – bronze, copper and iron, for example. Well, which running order here?

Part of the Ages problem, of course, is that they went on for so *long*. It's not your puny Age of the Video Recorder or Age of the Automated Telling Machine, or even your Age of Reason; it's hundreds and thousands of years at a stretch, when the climate changed just as much as the ornaments on your mantelpiece.

Oh, oh, still struggling over which came first, the bronze chicken or the iron egg? Don't bother to look it up; you'll only damage yourself – and disturb the dust – reaching up for that large and shamefully out-of-date encyclopaedia on the top shelf. This is how it was, OK – copper, bronze, iron. Yeah, yeah, we know you knew all the time; but in that case why did you never let *us* know? A postcard would have done . . . a phone call . . . you think all this head-banging stuff is *easy*?

Oh well, never mind, let's get back to the women; we hate to see such mutinous looks on fresh little faces. So . . . we've been ape-type creatures for some length of time, we may or may not then have gone bathing for another few million years. The next step is to go walkabout during the Ice Ages and become what is laughingly known as Homo Sapiens. No objections here, we hope, if for that term we substitute another one: viz. Wise Woman? At about 10,000 BC the ice-sheets melt away, and the climate, which, after all, has nowhere to go but up, becomes comparatively pleasant. Wisely, we frisk into the New Old Stone Age. At this point, Britain is still firmly joined to the continent of Europe.

QUIZ

Do you find in Britain's non-island status clues to:
(a) The Missing Link?
(b) The Fixed Link?
(c) The present hostility displayed to us by some of our European partners?

Ingenious! With a mind like that, what are you doing reading a book like this?

Now, ritual is already very important to us. The chaps dance around dressed as deer and the rest of us make female magic as carved idols and as flesh and blood women. We also all work pretty hard at our different chores. At this point you may want to refer back to your diary entry for Great-great-etc. Grandmama. Oh shame on you! Is yours the only one to skive off berry-picking and sit with her feet up on a fur rug eating a box of chocolates?

Best proceed with toute vitesse then to the Middle Stone Age when temperatures improved a bit more and we were cast adrift from Europe. (Don't clamour for details, *please*; that's all you're getting and that's that.)

Now comes an interesting bit. Round about 2,500 BC, the first boat-loads of immigrants turned up, some from northern France and the Low Countries, some from the Mediterranean, and some, more primitive, from Scandinavia. It's the New Stone Age already, and our astounded eyes fall for the first time on sheep, cattle and woven garments. Given that we seem to have existed largely on shell-fish for much of the Mid-Stone Age period, it seems likely that our stone implements, wielded with enthusiasm, also fell on these adventurous four-footed visitors.

However, ideas for recipes were not the only cultural gift of these first immigrants. Those with a Mediterranean origin were keen to pass on news and views about a Great Mother Goddess, in whose honour they constructed massive tombs, monuments and barrows. This was, amongst other things, the Age of the Megalith, as is shown by archaeological remains in the Cotswolds, New Grange, Kintyre and the Orkneys. The village of Skara Brae in Orkney (strictly speaking of early Bronze Age vintage, but at heart a Stone Age New Town) has presented itself to some eyes as being shaped in the very form of the Goddess.

And then there is Silbury Hill which has so far defied all attempts to give it an identity other than as a massive tribute to the Earth Mother. An old tradition of placing offerings of water, cakes and figs on the top of Silbury Hill continued into the first part of the eighteenth century. And when the glorious Anon once again picked up her pen to remind us of the things which we should be reminded about, she was perhaps thinking of this same mysterious spot.

> There was an old woman
> Lived under a hill
> And if she's not gone
> She lives there still.

ACTIVITY

Make a sketch of the kind of megalith which you would be proud to display in your garden or window-box.

Figures of the Goddess herself have been found in several places in Britain, including the early axe-factory of Grimes Graves in Norfolk. The Mediterranean fertility religion and the megalithic cult of the dead thrived, it seems, on dark, earth-bound chambers and other symbols of death and re-birth.

However, by 1800 BC, the end was in sight for the matriarchal peasant communities who worshipped the Earth Mother. These followers of the Old Religion – not, of course, that they knew at the time that it was soon to become Old – were overrun, dispossessed and enslaved by the misleadingly harmless-sounding Beaker Folk. Although Irish smiths had developed a copper industry some time before, it was these warlike Beakers, hailing from France and the Low Countries, who put the Bronze into Age. The dispossessed locals were small and dark; the invaders were tall, heavy and fair. Oh, you've seen that film too?

Self-check question

Whose side would you have been on?

The contribution of the Beakers didn't end at popularising bronze and slavery. They were a nomadic lot who believed in herding up not only their animals and slaves but also their women and children. The male head of a family group ruled over his own little

Mid Bronze Age in the Summer Country –
the Ancient maze of YNS WYTRYN*
hoof & horn… hoof & horn
Holy Grail, Mona! My thongs are dropping off… how much longer have we got to trek round?
Shhh Brigit! – have some respect…
Well.. we've been at it since May Eve… an invocation never used to take this long..
It's the world of men, innit? – You don't get the respect any more.. Anyway, listen… they've made CB contact!
BRIDESTONE BRENDA to RIDGEWAY RITA… ..do you copy?
We have a direct ley to Silbury, ma'am…
Thanks, Ceridwyn.. I'll take it in the cauldron
Yes.. mm mm..
..I see..
As we suspected, these sky gods will indeed be around for the forseeable future!
Quite some time, ha ha!
Put it down, Arthur!
Consequently, we propose to make fully operational the Hidden Mystery!
break break
Sisters! The priestesses of the Mother are going underground!
The Corridors of Annwn?
The Halls of Underworld?
Just stop it, Arthur!
Lately, it has been necessary for the Great Goddess to appear to hobnob with minor deities of the patriarchy..
So, when the Sky-god trinity is established…
no!
..we'll already have our moles on the inside!
Nuns! – The future's in nuns! Brides of Christ!
What?
Who?
?
Well, he's the son of the god.. born of a holy virgin, then slain for the good of all. His mother grieves for him, they eat his body & drink his blood ..& he resurrects!
It sounds amazing – but will it work?
How d'you like 'Hail Mary full of Grace, Queen of the Heavens?'!
Our work is done! It is time! – For Maiden to be Woman.. for Crone to seek rest!
Nay mothers, leave us not!
hoof & horn hoof & horn
all who die shall be reborn
Weep not daughters.. tis Her will..
keen keen weep
Arthur, put it away!!
Farewell! – Don't forget to feed the snakes, Brigit…
Alack! They sail to Avalon & sleep..
I said Iraklion on Crete, but I don't think they heard…
libation, madam?
When's the next horde due, Mavis?
GOLDEN STRING TAVERNA
LABYRINTH
GUIDE
KNOSSOS
BULL-LEAP
YOUR NAME HERE!
O, there's a good millennium to go yet…
Great hairy Theseus! – They can miniaturise anything these days!
* Glastonbury, for non-Welsh speakers

kingdom. Although the women shared much of the pastoral work and achieved status through childrearing, they were discouraged from applying for the senior executive posts.

However, in touching recognition that there must be *somebody* who knew even more than he did, Mr Beaker introduced to these happy isles the Indo-European concept of a 'Sky god'. For the first time, temples were built. The old deity had been worshipped at the megaliths and at large communal grave sites. The new one preferred worshippers to bury themselves in neat individual family mounds along with representations of their wealth – and to keep these gloomy things quite separate from his centres of devotion. Stonehenge – a major new development of this time – reached up to the sky and light, not down to the earth and darkness.

Self-check question

Has anything that's been said tempted you to change sides at all?

Round about 1700 BC, a further invasion of similar folk (the Pyrex People?) submerged Wessex in a positive deluge of nomadic warrior aristocrats. Some posh bits were added to Stonehenge and foreign trade was extended, though Egypt rather than Japan seems to have had the fashionable technology.

In between the waves of invasion, the old matriarchal peasants popped their heads out from time to time, particularly north of Watford. Gradually, they got even bolder and a merging of the different peoples took place. During a comparatively peaceful Mid-Bronze Age, the country became increasingly settled, though the great forests remained untouched. But by the time 1000 BC rolled round, wars in Europe and the Near East led to streams of merchants and refugees beaching up on our coasts, hotly pursued by the first wave of invading Celtic tribes.

QUIZ

Imagine that you are herding cattle by the sea-shore and happen upon a sister who is clearly a Celtic invader. Do you:

(a) ask her home for barley-cup tea?
(b) entreat her to save you from your lord and master?
(c) do a swift black-market currency deal?
(d) enquire as to the burial habits of her lot?
(e) compliment her on her jewellery?

Iron finally arrived about 450 BC and silicon-chipped the bronze industry. Nothing daunted, we continued to make great strides in technology (though military rather than domestic, surprise, surprise), trade and marketing. Living in small villages or hilltop strongholds, we expanded our social units somewhat and managed to exist pretty successfully without a highly privileged aristocratic class.

The Celtic warlords were, however, too much for us in the end. Between 300–200 BC, they swept over here, having paid particular attention to the brochures on Scotland,

Yorkshire and Cornwall, and brought with them the La Tène culture and other peculiar words. Glastonbury dates back to this period.

And then, about 75 BC, Belgic tribes helped us to further change the face of the country. We moved down from the hills into the valleys and started chopping down trees. We also spent a fair bit of time chopping down each other, being forced to act out our tribal feuds these many years before we could sublimate with 'Dallas'. Not surprisingly, blood sacrifice à la Druid was the religious order of the day.

Jane Bridge
Joyce Wethered
Sport
Lillian Board Athletics
Mary Rand Athletics
Tessa Sanderson Javelin
Wendy Norman Pentathlete
Amy Johnson. Solo Aviator. d. 1941
Mary Peters Pentathlon & Community Sports
Clare Francis Solo Yachtswoman
Rachel Heyhoe-Flint. Cricketer
Winifred Spooner Air Racer & private Pilot d. 1933
Sharron Davies. Swimmer
Sonia Lannaman. Sprinter
Phyllis Lauder Table Tennis
Mandy Fisher Pro Snooker player
Pitman
Liz Hobbs Water-Ski Racer
Fatima Whitbread. Javelin
Charlotte Cooper 1st Olympic Gold Medallist
Jenny Racehorse Trainer
Lucinda Greene 3-Day Event world champ.
Dot Crowley, 1929 Speedway Rider
Kitty Godfree Wimbledon ch. 1924, 26
Joyce Smith Marathon
Lorna Boothe. Hurdles
Jayne Torvill Ice Dancer
Julie Tullis Everest Mountaineer
Body Builder
Carolyn Cheshire
Mandy Jones. Cyclist
Virginia Wade Wimbledon ch. 1977
Sarah Potter. Duchess of Bedford. Kathy Taylor. Gillian Sheen
Beryl Burton. Lady 'Granny' Arran. Dorothy Hyman

MODULE 2

The Romans in Britain

Bread and circuses, did you say? Don't make me laugh. These were all right for their own plebs back in Rome; but us lot were not only fearsome and barbarous but ungrateful as well. Frankly, we didn't want to get civilised.

QUIZ

Which would you prefer:
(a) a nice new plumbing job – hot-and-cold, the works?
(b) sticking to the old Celtic mysteries?

Go on, admit it – you've gone for (a). Decadent lot. Remember the Fall of Rome. Haven't you ever considered the possibility that there was more to that than hanky-panky in the locker-rooms and over-emphasis on violin practice? Don't you think that excessive cleanliness may have played its part? Well, if you're going to sulk, it's back to the Romans, I suppose. Now, we know all about the chaps. They wore togas, spoke to tables and other inanimate objects, and enjoyed a spot of rape and pillage. When they were soldiers (which seemed to be often), they worried about things which didn't even make sense in English, far less in Latin. Take the Latin noun, *moles,* for example. A teacher of our youth, a woman determined to follow history's straighter paths, insisted on translating this word as 'mole' rather than as the unappealing but more intelligible 'massive breakwater'. She would then proceed to describe to a goggle-eyed class how, at the drop of a helmet, Roman soldiers would set to and throw up these self-same moles. We found that a profoundly impressive aspect of their lives. After all, if they threw up moles, what on earth did they manage to keep down?

Roman women, as far as we know, refrained from throwing up moles, furry or stony. However, they shared other challenges with their men folk. And when we say 'challenges', we mean counting in Roman numerals and keeping their verbs to the end of sentences. It's no wonder really that the Romans had to bathe such a lot: the tepidarium was probably the best place to work out their sentences in advance – not to mention using all their fingers and toes for counting.

Ladies and gents didn't all wallow in together, as some of you may be glad to hear. You know the kind of thing: X a.m.–II p.m. men, III p.m.–VI p.m. women. No, smartass, it was a *deliberate* mistake: the men did indeed have longer hours in which to ablute, think, and so on. Separate bedrooms too, dears; but please don't ask how the rota system worked there – all in all, we'd rather go back to the moles.

IF IT'S TUESDAY, IT MUST BE GAUL...

* Daughters of the Republic

DOR ROMA CHAPTER

CAPITOLINE TOURS inc

WOAD

true blue

HAIL, DAUGHTER!
GREETINGS FROM **BRITAIN**, OUTPOST OF **EMPIRE!**
- LIFE SURE HAS OPENED UP SINCE I **DIVORCED**
YOUR FATHER. WELL, WE LAND AT DOVER, &
CHECK OUT **DUTY FREE**. YOU SHOULD SEE THE **RINSE** I GOT FROM THIS BRITISH **WOAD!** ANYWAY,

THE **TOUR** OPERATOR SAYS WE HAVE TO SEE THIS
LONDINIUM. WELL, YOU KNOW WHAT THEY SAY,
WE CAME, WE SAW, WE **LEFT!** - IS **IT** THE **PITS!**
FINALLY, WE MADE IT TO **BATH**. DID WE **NEED** ONE!

WE'RE BOOKED INTO A KINDA **STATELY VILLA** -
STAYING WITH **LOCAL BRITISH ARISTOS**. VERY NICE.
BUT THEY JUST DON'T UNDER**STAND** CENTRAL
HEATING OVER HERE. IT'S ENOUGH TO **FREEZE**
THE **TOGA** OFF OF **ZEUS**. BRITS NEVER **WILL** PUT
THE HYPOCAUST ONTO **FULL**. SURE IS NO PLACE
LIKE **ROME**! .. THE **WOMEN** HERE ARE **DESPERATE** FOR HOT FASHION NEWS. & I CAN SEE WHY!

KEEP BRITAIN TIDY - TAKE YOUR LITTER HOME

roman imperialists out now

I **MEAN**, SOME OF THE **GUYS** HERE WEAR THESE
WEIRD **TUBES** ON THEIR LEGS! - THE TOUR COMPANY
HAS A **RENT-A-LITTER** CONCESSION & WE ALL GET
AROUND JUST **FINE**. IT'S REALLY KINDA **QUAINT** -
THOUGH SOME OF THE LOCAL **PLEBS** DON'T LOOK
TOO HAPPY. GUESS IT'S DOWN TO ALL THAT **RAIN**.

I MEET THE **GIRLS** AT THE **BATHS** - HOT TUB,
SCRAPE DOWN, MASSAGE - A **HEAVY SESSION** IN
THE **PARLOUR**. THEN ME & SOME OF THE **MATRONS**
STOP OVER AT THE **TEMPLE** TO WORK OUT A FEW
CURSES. ARE THEY **MEAN** HERE! - OR
MAYBE WE HIT THE SHOPPING MALL. - Y'KNOW
- IRISH **LINEN**, BRITISH **TWEEDS** - CUTE **DRUID** STUFF - **HEY!** - I GOT A WHOLE **BUNCH** OF NATIVE
JEWELLRY. **VERY** MACHO. GETTING **TOURISTY**,
THOUGH - FAKE CELTIC **RITUALS**, TACKY
SOUVENIRS - SASSY SLAVES - **RIP OFFS** - I
HAVE TO **GO**. WE HAVE AN ETHNIC BRITISH **ORGY**
SCHEDULED FOR TONIGHT, & ANYWAY, THE
SCRIBE'S GETTING **CRAMP**. HAIL, FAREWELL -
& HAVE A NICE **DAY**, NOW! **MA**

Self-check question

Mole: who she?

In case you think that the grandeur that was Rome deserves better than this, let's turn to a consideration of Romano-British religion. Sulis Minerva had a temple dedicated to her at that popular spot, Aquae Sulis ('Bath' to you). She left a splendid head of herself to be discovered in the Great Bath in the eighteenth century; and, frankly, we wouldn't be surprised if she took that plunge in shame at the paltry requests being made of her. Perhaps you've heard of the Bath Curses? (Good on you!) And maybe you thought they were of the type to send anyone rushing in terror to the nearest cloaca?

ACTIVITY

(kick your shoes off – this is the fun bit)
Think of the person you hate most in the whole world. Explain why, then describe precisely and in minute detail the scenario which you would like Minerva to arrange for him (whoops! sorry, we meant 'them'). Don't take more than two hours to complete this activity; and, if you happened to get a little over-excited, please remember to leave the room as you would wish to find it.

Feeling better? OK, now perhaps you'd like to compare your glorious effort with the following mean-minded and inhibited curses found at Aquae Sulis.

> The name of
> the culprit
> who has stolen
> my bracelet
>
> I have given to the goddess Sulis
> the six silver pieces which I have lost
> It is for the goddess to exact it
> from the debtors written below;
> Senecianus and Saturninus
> and Anniola. The draft has been copied.
> Anniola
> Senecianus
> Saturninus

Call that grandeur, eh? Mind you, there's a strange and impressive ring about another one discovered there:

> May he who carried off Vilbia from
> Me become as liquid as water.
> (May) she who obscenely devoured
> her (become) dumb whether Velvinnia
> Exsuperuus, Verianus,
> Severinus, Augustalis,
> Comitianus, Catusminiamus,
> Germanilla (or) Jovina.

Now *there* was a challenge worthy of Minerva, don't you think?

Well, enough of these Roman invaders, with their soppy baths and cissy curses. Let's turn now to the Cantii from Canterbury, the Regni from Chichester, the Belgae from Winchester, the Coritani from Leicester, the Brigantes from Yorkshire – and the Iceni from East Anglia. If, like us, you suspect that your roots lie in the rough trade of history, then get ready to feel at home. And – yes, you've guessed it – raise a hand across the centuries to Boudicca (or Boadicea, what you will), Queen of the Iceni.

When Britain was made a Roman province, it remained for some years under the direct rule of the governor. Certain tribes, however, including the Iceni, managed to avoid this fate by retaining their native princes to act as client-kings of Rome. Prasatages, King of the Iceni (and husband of Boudicca), managed to sustain what is usually called a long and prosperous reign until, that's life, he died. Although Prasatages left a will making the Roman Emperor co-heir along with Prasatages' own two daughters (thus hoping to safeguard his kingdom from attack), the Romans had had enough of friendly treaties by this point (AD 60) and decided to treat the kingdom as though it had been conquered.

You don't need to stretch your imaginations too much to picture the kind of treatment handed out to the Iceni. Boudicca was flogged. Her daughters were raped. The chiefs were deprived of their estates; the king's relatives were treated like slaves.

This was the woman they flogged, in the words of a Roman historian, Dio Cassius: 'She was huge of frame, terrifying of aspect, and with a harsh voice. A great mass of bright red hair fell to her knees.' And if that's how the Romans described her, imagine how she really looked.

Fearing that worse was to come, Boudicca led the Iceni in an uprising against the Romans, soon joined by the Trinobantes who were having a rough time in Colchester. Cunningly waiting until most of the occupying army was occupied in wiping out the Druids in Anglesey, the Britons attacked Colchester, a sensible choice since it had no walls. Omens were seen – or, if they weren't, the old British propaganda machine was already finely tuned and in fighting form. The statue of victory in Colchester fell down (for no apparent reason) with its head turned as if fleeing the enemy. At the mouth of the Thames, a phantom settlement was seen in ruins; the sea turned blood red; and the ebb tide left behind on the sand shapes like corpses.

QUIZ

Imagine that you were an ancient Briton seeing such sights. Would you:

(a) march forward, whooping
(b) forswear strong liquor forthwith
(c) run like hell in the opposite direction?

So it's to be (c), is it? No wonder we're in the mess we are. Still, at least you're honest.

Our ancestors, of course, chose (a), thinking it all looked pretty good. Which it did for a while. Colchester fell like a pancake and the imperial agent withdrew to Gaul. Meanwhile, the Roman governor laid off the Druids and returned sharp-ish to Londinium – only to make a tactical retreat when faced with the British hordes. The same hordes stormed Londinium and Verulanium (St Albans), with deaths from both sides amounting to something like 70,000. The Britons, according to Tacitus, the Roman historian, did not take prisoners; they cut throats, burned and crucified.

But the main Roman army was waiting, re-grouped in the Midlands. Before the final battle, Boudicca is said to have driven round all the tribes in a chariot with her daughters in front of her. She is also reported to have made the following speech:

> We British are used to women commanders in war. I am descended from mighty men! But now I am not fighting for my kingdom and wealth. I am fighting as an ordinary person for my lost freedom, my bruised body, and my outraged daughters. Nowadays Roman rapacity does not even spare our bodies. Old people are killed, virgins raped. But the gods will grant us the vengeance we deserve! The Roman division which dared to fight is annihilated. The others cower in their camps, or watch for a chance to escape. They will never face even the din and roar of all our thousands, much less the shock of our onslaught. Consider how many of you are fighting and why! Then you will win this battle or perish. That is what I, a woman, plan to do! – let the men live in slavery if they will.

The tribes didn't come up to scratch. Roman military *nous* resulted in a massacre of horrendous proportions; it has been estimated that almost 80,000 Britons fell, as against 400 Roman dead. Boudicca escaped but to avoid capture killed herself by taking poison; the fate of her daughters is unrecorded.

Nero, the Roman Emperor of the time, subsequently recognised that the harshness and injustice of the regime in Britain had played a large part in causing the uprising and he instituted a milder administration.

Legend has it that Boudicca is buried under Platform 9 of King's Cross station, the putative site of that last, ghastly battle.

MODULE 3

Not the Knights of the Round Table or *Ladies and Lakes*

What do people like about games? Is it the sublimated urge to humiliate if not kill? The desire to prove that the school chess club was being absurdly short-sighted when it suggested that you take up Snap? Or it is just the pleasure of not having to make conversation?

We ask because, frankly, we don't like games much and so have devised a diversion particularly suitable for non-players and chronic kibitzers. In our game you don't even have to go so far as to shake a dice; we've done all these boring bits already. So, relax, read on: this time you can't lose.

Our game, 'Ladies and Lakes', is a variant on other role-playing fantasy games. Especially if you number amongst your acquaintance some rich, power-mad, competitive and obsessive men, you may be familiar with the basic elements of such games. Out of wargaming, by Tolkien, they tend to be played against elaborate medieval backgrounds, bristling with traps, monsters, witches and aggressive wandering fighters. Like living in an inner city. The idea is that you take on the role of a medieval character and then join others in some daft quest, falling into assorted adventures and temptations on the way. Everything is directed by a referee, another player who has designed the scenario and does the sound effects. Fancy dice are thrown constantly to direct the outcome of almost everything. Chance plays a huge part in all this, but, then, doesn't it always?

As you'll see, our game shares some of these elements; but we've tampered wholesale with the environment, made all the decisions and cut out the middlemen.

So ... welcome again to the world of Camelot. You remember the bare bones of the received version? Sprightly young Arthur, seemingly of relatively humble origin, is in reality a royal sprig under the tutelage of the wizard Merlin. He comes out as such by proving himself the only young gentleman capable of yanking an enchanted sword out of an enchanted stone. Once crowned, Arthur feels the lack of a sword of his own but soon acquires the terrific Excalibur from the white-samite-clad arm of the Lady of the Lake; in return, she later asks him for the head of one of his errant knights. Having got hold of a sword, Arthur clearly must next get married. He chooses Guinevere, despite warnings from Merlin that she won't be good for him and, anyway, will be loved by his best friend, Lancelot.

The bride brings Arthur a Round Table but also a load of trouble, just as wise Merlin predicted. What with his weirdo sister, Morgan Le Fay, uttering dark curses and imprecations all over the court, and with Guinevere proving very prone to abduction by nasty men and rescue by nice Lancelot, Arthur's life is soon made a positive misery by difficult women. How can he concentrate on the important things of life, like jousting and fighting for real?

The phantom Holy Grail proves a blessing in disguise, scattering the knights round the countryside in quest of the Real Thing. Being in a state of sin on account of shenanigans with Guinevere, poor Lancelot cannot join in the fun; instead, he confesses all to a hermit and lurks, chastely, in an isolated spot until he can return to court.

A trifle depleted, battered and bruised, the company of knights returns to Camelot. Old fraternal quarrels are resumed but are soon overshadowed by the shocking revelation that for many years the Queen has been betraying the King with the gallant Lancelot. Lancelot makes a violent escape from court, returns to save Guinevere from execution and then becomes involved in sieges, counter-sieges and lengthy negotiations on the fate of the hapless Queen. All agree that the saddest aspect of the whole affair is the break-up of the Brotherhood.

In the end, Arthur is mortally wounded in internecine battle, uses an inefficient knightly courier service to return Excalibur to the Lady of the Lake, and is then borne away in a barge by three weeping queens (no, *not* members of the Brotherhood). Guinevere becomes a nun; while Lancelot returns to the life of a hermit.

Or so They have said ... Now join us in our women's quest to reach Avalon, a place of Old Magic, relatively unscathed.

IGRAYNE casts an unpretentious haemorrhoid spell on MERLIN MORGAN sends VIVIANE a note in a bottle; they throw, & move on to an ancient GROVE...
'TIS SACRED TO THE LADY, & OBEYS NOT THE LAW OF MAN...
..WHICH IS WHY, WHEN WE COME OUT, WE STEP STRAIGHT INTO ARTHUR'S COURT, SEVERAL YEARS HENCE...
..in short, there's not a more convenient spot... than CAMELOT!
CASTING A GLAMOUR OF INVISIBILITY OVER OURSELVES!
Not your Richard Harris impression again..
THEY'RE HEAVILY INTO CHIVALRY & MANLY PURITY..
If I slay one more dragon, I'll scream..
REEK
pong
whiff
OH REALLY? -THROW THE DICE!!
LISTEN, ARTHUR, HOMEOPATHY'S ALL VERY WELL, BUT ME AND THE LADS THINK IT'S ABOUT TIME YOU GOT MARRIED!
WELL, IF YOU THINK I SHOULD..
..I'LL HAVE GUINEVERE!
?!
HER OR NOT AT ALL!
THAT WOMAN'S UNWHOLESOME! -SHE'LL ONLY INFLAME MEN'S LUSTS & BRING NAUGHT BUT STRIFE!
Bad Luck! GUINEVERE has thrown 'marry ARTHUR' - Instantly, she finds herself back at her PA'S house, being proposed to by proxy.
WHO THE HELL'S PROXY?
THE KING, LADY, DESIRETH THY HAND..
YANK
Actually, this is SIR LANCELOT, & he desireth a lot more than this. G. throws to see if she's in favour... She's not. However! - as a Wedding Present..
DADDY! HOW SWEET! A ROUND TABLE AND 100 MATCHING KNIGHTS!
I HATE DINNER PARTIES..
..& WHAT'S WRONG WITH A TOASTER?
Magic Fails! At the altar, G. suffers a near-fatal MINUS 10 damage points!
I DOooo...
G's weakened state renders her prey to almost constant abduction...
In fact, a Petty Tyrant turns up on a WANDERING MONSTER throw
As Queen's Champion, L. rescues G., who throws to see whether or not to be lovers with him. She throws 'NOT..'
LOOK! I DON'T ACTUALLY MEAN ANYTHING BY THIS..
Back at CAMELOT, MORGAN throws, & challenges MERLIN to combat!
druid
CALL YOURSELF A DRUID???
QUIET, THEY'LL HEAR YOU!
Druid?
THEY'RE SUPPOSED TO - YOU FRAUD!
-Another WANDERING MONSTER throw! Turning up a party of fighting CLERICS
..& THAT BREEZE CONSTANTLY FLUTTERING THROUGH YOUR BEARD DOESN'T IMPRESS ME! YOU MIGHT HAVE STOLEN THE HOLY SWORD & SCABBARD-
rummage
root
- BUT YOU WON'T GET-
THIS!!
CURSES! THE SACRED VESSEL CUNNOG!
the GRAIL!
grail!
THE GRAIL!

WOULDN'T YOU KNOW.. THEY THINK IT'S PART OF THEIR CHRISTIAN REGALIA..
an angel took the GRAIL...
find it!
WELL, LET'S SPLIT BEFORE THE ECSTASY WEARS OFF!
3 Throws later..
GUINEVERE!
AT LAST!
I THREW A DIVORCE! CAMELOT'S EMPTY- IF THEY'RE NOT OFF QUESTING FOR THE GRAIL, THEY'RE FIGHTING AMONG THEMSELVES...
A successful throw. VIVIANE is met on the road.
BLESSED BE, DAUGHTERS..
HAIL, MOTHER- IS AVALON NIGH?
A TRAP!
THE DEMON KING, I PRESUME..
POING
PAFF!
SHOW RESPECT, WOMAN!
IT'S THE END FOR YOUR LOT - YOUR ARCANE, SUBVERSIVE IDEAS! — GUINEVERE WANDERING AROUND THE COUNTRYSIDE WHEN SHE SHOULD BE AT HOME, FORNICATING WITH LANCELOT & GIVING EVERY-BODY DECENT EXCUSES FOR STARTING UP INTRIGUES & VENDETTAS!
TOUGH!
-ANYWAY,- I WANT THAT GRAIL!
POWER MAD..
Weakened by this orgy of self-indulgence MERLIN is easily dealt with...
YOUR NATURAL SUPERIORITY'S TOO MUCH FOR ME, O MERLIN - IT'S IN THERE...
fool...
MERLIN, trapped by his own greed & VIVIANE's superior power, suffers maximum damage points. He is left to expire.
IT'S NOT!
IT'S TRUE - THEY'RE ALL AT WAR WITH EACH OTHER..
CHIVALRY & PURITY NOT FLAVOUR OF THE MONTH?
IT WON'T STOP WHILE ARTHUR'S GOT EXCALIBUR & THE SCABBARD- HOWEVER MUCH HE BLEEDS, WEARING THAT, HE WON'T DIE..
& on a daring throw, MORGAN enters ARTHUR'S tent & reclaims the SCABBARD..
Z
Soon, he sustains a mortal wound
A WANDERING MONSTER throw
C'MON, GUINEVERE.. YOU KNOW YOU REALLY WANT IT!
CLONG
GNNG
ONCE & FOR ALL, LANCELOT, SOD OFF!
L. retires. In disgust, he becomes a HERMIT
..Finally - the LAKE of AVALON!
RIGHT- THROW FOR THE SEATING PLAN
*Players now share a 3000 pt. spiritual BONUS
YOU'VE GOT THE CORACLE, VIVIANE -WE'RE IN THE BARGE...
ARTHUR nears DEATH...
snatch!
...A last throw - & the BARGE must turn back..
you can tell she's done this sort of thing before..
I KNEW IT - TEARS BEFORE BEDTIME...
Sorry, mum...

MODULE 4

The Bio Tapestry

You know already, of course, that that Other Tapestry – the Bayeux one – abounds in men, hawks, hounds and funny griffin creatures. Guess how many women are in it. Oh, go on. 60? 50? *30*? Higher? Lower? In fact, the correct answer is 3. *Three*. Were you even *warm*?

Well, we Brits certainly started off in the way we intended to continue. Scholarly word has it, however (this is true – so was the number 3), that the embroiderers who worked on the designs may well have been female.

A tale cannot resist hanging thereon . . .

THE:BAYEUX:TAPESTRY
A:LONDON ADVERTISING AGENCY C:1090 AD.
...& ideally, when I've had enough, I'll get out & do my own stuff..
JOB NO: 1066
CLIENT: BISHOP ODO of BAYEUX
FV&S Personal Promotion...
campaign Spearhead PROMO VIDEO...
right.. it pays the rent but is it art?
..& since the late King's demise, Client's been anxious that his role in events of the recent past - the Invasion... Hastings.. y'know.. should be displayed on permanent record..
...touch of creative shading & positive highlighting?
right..
FREEMAN, VILLEIN & SERF:
Well, team - I have to say - Client loves it! - great video!
LEGAL DECENT HONEST & TRUTHFUL
heh - great embroidery!
Incredible balance! Client's image enhanced - very tasty - pops up in all the right places.. Harold - honourable guy who went too far - William - tough but fair - Man in white hat. Conquered. Love it.
Fantastic concept, Chas.. really great.. Knockout artwork & classic cartooning ... Ace job.
Uh.. Triffic, Ed!
Got some plonk, have we?
Lovely tight writing Kev... lean, honed, punchy! - Nice bit of irony....
Cheers, Ed!
Irony?!
Spot-on market research. We've got all the punters on one shot.... Peasant, Baron, King.
-really answers the brief. S'great! Immediate, accessible graphic images sell Client subliminally to the Cs, Ds, & Es...
..& an immaculate aesthetic grabs the A's & B's by the short & curlies!
Lovely stuff, these borders.. little bit cheeky.. little bit surreal - but not too jokey! Nice one!
We have ourselves a very happy Client..
..And triffic workmanship, eh Ed? Aethelwynn & the girls really came up with the goods!
Yeah... Aethelwynn & the girls...
Anything wrong, Mr. Freeman?
You may not know it - but I always carry...
My Norman Army Art Director's Special Penknife.
- And it's a damn good job I do!
whip
I thought I'd made it clear to everybody.
a) this is not a piece of political advertising - & b) Embroiderers, Illuminators, Any bloody artists - you watch them every step of the bloody way!
Get the invisible menders, Roger...
Yes, SIR!
THE:UNDERSIGNED:DO:PROTEST:AGAINST:
I: GLORIFICATION OF WAR & 'VIDEO NASTY' ELEMENTS IN THIS WORK:
II: THE DERISORY PORTRAYAL OF WOMEN: (ONLY 3, AND AS VICTIM)
III: HEAVY IMPLICATIONS OF WHITE = GOOD & POLITICALLY OK HAIRDOS:
IIII: UNEQUAL PAY & LOUSY CONDITIONS:
:(SIGNED) AETHELWYNN & THE WOMEN:

Jobs for Women
When I joined, they said I could do hard news...
PLAY-TIME
A
4 · Mediaperson
Jobs for Women
...You've re-invented the wheel, then..
5 · Potter
Jobs for Women
Bloody Solid fuel..
6 · Peasant

ALL THAT..
4. Mrs. Pepys' Diary
DOWN THERE
1655. I, ELIZABETH ST. MICHEL, AT 15 YEARS, MARRIED SAMUEL PEPYS, 29, CIVIL SERVANT. FOUND SPOT.
MONDAY. BORED WITLESS. SAMUEL SAYS I'M FRIVOLOUS, EXTRAVAGANT, EASILY ROUSED TO ANGER & SULKS. WHO WOULDN'T BE?? THERES NOTHING TO DO. SUSPECT SAMUEL OF FORNICATING.
your Husband stays away tonight?
aye, if his promotion hastens along...
WEDNESDAY. S. THINKS ME SEXUALLY COLD. I AM RACKED WITH MONTHLY PAINS, ACHES & GROWTHS. & S. STINKS. BOUGHT PAIR OF DRAWERS.
Madam! Thour't not going out in them?
TOLD S. OF LUSTFUL PROPOSITION FROM EARL OF SANDWICH. REFUSED. HIM A PEER, TOO...
'tis all the rage at court...
S. SUSPECTS ME OF FORNICATION! (IT BEING MY DAY FOR THE DANCING MASTER!) I KNOW, BECAUSE HE WATCHED ME UNDRESS HOPING TO FIND ME WITHOUT MY DRAWERS! SHALL TELL DEB THERE IS MORE THAN ONE USE IN WEARING THEM!
DIARY
TODAY, I DISCOVER DEB WILLET, MY COMPANION, AS SHE COMB'D PEPYS' HAIR, ALLOWING HIM ACCESS TO FONDLE HER PERSON!! DEMANDED HER INSTANT REMOVAL. SLEPT WITH PEPYS.
& I'll bet she's not wearing any drawers!
3 WEEKS LATER, & DEB ONLY JUST GONE! PEPYS ON BEST BEHAVIOUR. BOUGHT NEW NIT COMB.
GUILT..

MODULE 5

The Middle Ages or *Are we half-way there?*

As many of you will be only too well aware, history gets harder as it goes on. Take the question of Ages, for example. In a rough and ready way most of us can cope with the idea of an Age being made of stone, iron, etc. – but what does it mean when you get a whole lot lumped together and called Dark, Middle, and so on? Darker than *what,* you may ask; and Middle *of* what? Are the Middle Ages the middle of history, for instance? And in that case will they become the One-Third Ages as history gets longer?

We hate to disappoint you, but we intend to refrain from shedding any light at all on the Dark Ages. This is because we shrink from the name Matilda and also from a close examination of the life of people who found it natural to discuss the price of butter in Anglo-Saxon.

ACTIVITY

Take two minutes for free association. What adjectives does the name 'Matilda' suggest to you? In what ways would such traits/attributes render the holder of the name suitable/unsuitable for the throne of England?

Now, the Middle Ages are a different matter. Quite apart from being much brighter altogether, they contain some enthralling mysteries as well as far fewer women called Matilda. For a start, there's the question of headgear. You'll recognise the three classic looks:

1. The coif
2. The two-horned number
3. The cone with dangler

QUIZ

Concentrating your intellectual energies on no. 3, would you explain its popularity by pointing to:

(a) its usefulness if a lady should happen upon a swarm of bees?

(b) its historical significance as the first, miniaturised, maypole, from which sprang women's vital role in Merrie England?

(c) its capacity to add inches to the stature without forcing the lady into high heels?

Ah ha, so we have a major revolt here? Women being forced to conform to men's bizarre sexual fantasies, did somebody say? And another voice explaining that the fashion industry has always embodied the nexus of patriarchal projections with capitalist opportunism? Now listen, you last lot, just wait until capitalism has been invented (see p. 4,977) before casting your stones. And as for you others – if you want the heavy stuff, you'll get the heavy stuff. God, consumerism has a lot to answer for; does nobody take pleasure in the little things of life any more?

All right, forget the headgear. Sorry we brought it up in the first place. Just who's being childish, might we ask? Oh pooh to you too, sister. Yes, OK, rigorous intellectual debate and all that; arguments ad feminam dismissed out of court; kiss and make up; sisterhood conquers all. Let's get on, shall we?

We *were* talking about enthralling medieval mysteries, the first of which is headgear. The second is the status of women. If being presented at one moment as the main gate to hell and at the next as second sister to the gracious Queen of Heaven seems old hat to you now, it was fairly newly minted stuff then. (For a full discussion of old hats, see above). You may be familiar too with a third element of the plot, which is a general lack of cultural acknowledgment that most of these angels/devils in fact spent the greatest part of their time slogging away in fields and workshops just like their menfolk did. (The rest of their time they spent in trivial feminine pursuits like keeping house and making cloth.)

Courtly love was, of course, an exclusive offer tailored to a pretty narrow target market. If you lacked husband or castle, then you could forget it. But if you had these requisites, then you could step straight into a pretty weird scene, devised in the south of France during the last half of the twelfth century.

The package on offer was as follows:

- a knight (unmarried), desperate to pander to your every whim
- songs of praise and love devised by same knight

Your part of the deal involved:

- giving knight a golden ring, chaste kiss and sundry favours
- leading him merry hell through disdain, tests of love, etc.
- listening to the bloody songs.

ACTIVITY

Complete the following sentence in 10 words or less. Knight says to Lady, 'Do me a favour, love'; Lady replies, '**************'

In fact, married ladies of high estate didn't have to be stuck in this scenario. As landowners, they were people of great importance, even though their married state meant that their property rights fell into their husbands' hands for as long as the marriage lasted. Because these husbands tended to be away from home a good deal of the time – killing foreigners, scheming at court, etc. – the wives had to be capable of managing the estates in their absence. This could mean supervising the home farm; organising, without the help of J. Sainsbury, the smooth running of a vast household; collecting a ransom for the lord; and defending the castle against armed attackers. A lot more interesting, you may feel, than listening to some callow youth give a daily report on his emotional and spiritual progress.

Sliding down the social scale a bit (funny, isn't it, how natural that feels?), we come to working women. All unmarried women on the lower rungs worked for their living; and most married women also followed a trade or calling. Married women could even become unmarried women for the purpose of business: *femmes soles* was the designation given not only to unmarried women and widows but also to wives pursuing a trade separate to that of their husbands.

Self-check question

Are you quite clear in your own mind as to the differences between (a) sole bonne femme (b) femmes soles and (c) Dover sole?

Could you explain these differences on a television quiz show?

In the towns, girls as well as boys were apprenticed to trades, swearing as part of their contract that they would not get married, frequent taverns or rob their master/mistress of more than six pence a year. Women were involved in nearly all the crafts of the time, showing up as butchers, chandlers, net-makers, shoemakers, haberdashers, skinners, bookbinders, gilders, painters, silk-weavers, spicers, smiths and goldsmiths. At times, various guilds – the unions of the day – inveighed against the employment of any women other than the wives and daughters of members. The continued prevalence of women working in most trades – along with the continued low pay for these workers – seems to suggest that the guilds were as short-sighted, ineffectual and prejudiced in such matters as later brothers proved to be.

In both town and countryside, women played a major role in the textile industries and in the production and distribution of food and drink. In addition, country women took full part in agricultural labour – planting peas and beans, weeding, reaping, binding, threshing, winnowing, and so on.

Young Gentlemen wishing they hadn't gone 'slumming'

Needless to say, troubadours sang no poignant lays to women toiling in the fields and trafficking in ships. Such women tended to get the 'mouth of hell' version of their place in the world. One hopes that Chaucer's Wife of Bath was not alone in fighting a stalwart rearguard action against this gruesome ecclesiastical stuff. When husband no. 5 (no, *not* Bath himself) persisted in regaling her with nightly readings from a book 'of wikked wyves', she ripped out some of the offending pages and whacked him one on the chops. He retaliated, but in the end was no match for her determination to redress the balance of power in this particular marriage.

Not all women shared the Wife of Bath's relish in marriage as a glorious battlefield. Some chose to go into nunneries. Others went, but had little choice in the matter: for girls from the upper classes, a career as a nun was the only alternative to marriage. In the Middle Ages, it seems, girls from the lower classes were never Called and hence, conveniently, never became a financial burden on the Church. Sometimes, though, they could be *half*-Called, so to speak, and in that case they became lay sisters; but that was OK because they could then get on and do the dirty work with joy in their hearts.

QUIZ

Assuming that you're a young woman from an upper-crust family – oh, go on, make an effort – would you prefer to:

(a) get heavily into feudal law as a means of defending your estates?
(b) listen, with an enigmatic smile, to a boy's regular music practice?
(c) become a career nun, with your sights set on outwitting the bishop?

No, no, of course there's nothing peculiar about you. Well, not *really* peculiar. . . . Well. . . .

Returning swiftly to the nuns, let us first point out that throughout the Middle Ages, the occupants of nunneries were remarkably good at getting out of them. Despite thundering prohibitions from bishops – and even from Rome – nuns would sail forth from their convents for business trips, pilgrimages, visits to potentially sick relatives, and so on. After a visit by their bishop to present them with a copy of a Papal Bull forbidding nearly all contact with the outside world, some nuns from Lincoln pursued the eminent man to the gate, chucked the Bull at his head and yelled that no way were they going to take any notice of it.

Discipline was supposed to be strict, of course; but a lot depended on the temperament of the abbess or prioress. If she was a sociable type – as many of them seem to have been – then she and her nuns soon got on easy terms with the world outside. Even the inside world – in the person of aristocratic lady boarders – offered much scope for secular gregariousness. Fashion news was exchanged – the nuns making a creditable attempt to adapt their costume accordingly – and the ladies all complimented each other over quite extraordinary collections of pet animals. Monkeys, dogs, rabbits and birds were amongst the convent-dwelling creatures inveighed against, ineffectually, by innumerable bishops and archbishops.

These episcopal gentlemen made periodic visits to the nunneries in order to check up on behaviour. In private audience with the bish, each nun was given the opportunity to moan about things and tell tales on her sisters. It was not uncommon for an unpopular prioress to be accused of pawning the best silver. At times when they were all breaking the rules, however, the sisters would gang up together against the Very Revd Holmes and keep their own counsel about life in the convent.

Rules required that silence be observed for long stretches of the day; however, the nuns were allowed to use a system of signs to communicate with each other. Dinner time must often have been a lively affair. A sister wanting fish would 'wag her hands displaying sidelings in manner of a fish tail'; for mustard, another would 'hold her nose in the upper part of her right fist and rub it'; her neighbour, gasping for a drop of wine, would 'move her forefinger up and down the end of thumb afore her eye'. Perhaps the most intriguing sign was reserved for the sacristan who had just realised that she had not provided incense for the Mass. She would 'put her two fingers into her nostrils'.

Convent Kitchen
Sister Euphemia to see you, Mistress Bridges...
'Ow can I 'elp you, sister?
thank you, Ruby..
?
Oo - I 'ates that Rule of Silence.. last time, she ordered whole pig in jelly for the lady abbess's elevenses... turned out she only wanted a couple of ginger nuts..
shame, innit?
Sorry, dear - sounds like what? - Fish? Fish off? - The fish his hoff?
Bishop! the bishop coming?
Lor! An' there's nuffink ready!
That'll do, Ruby! & I'll be wanting that cauldron directly!
Now... I could give them my special jugged steak...
Or your special stuffed swan, Mistress B! - We 'aven't 'ad no swan for hever such a long time..
nasty great beaks, swans 'ave...
Ruby, that's sufficient! Go & see what the sister's trying to say!
Sister says Sister Gertrude got some wild boar yesterday in the hunt...
Cor! - 'As she got a dispensation, then?
No... she's always been like that...
Well, then! We can 'ave a nice bit o' brawn shaped up a bit exotic ... a cathedral, 'im being a bishop..
French too, eh?
'Ows it goin' up there, Daisy?
The pike rissoles went down ever so well..
So did Sister Beatitude's Fine Old Peculiar! I've 'ad to put two more barrels on!
Cor! Them nuns can't 'arf put it away!
Ruby! Wash your mouth out! ... & don't drop them gilded apples!
That's that! They've 'ad the centrepiece ...the Virgin bein' Annunciated in a toad in the hole grotto...
Time to put me feet up!
..Not you, Ruby me gel!
..An what's the matter with you, Rose?
Maybe I shouldn't be sayin' it, Mistress B, but the way that there bishops been stuffin' imself.. well.. it ain't decent ... not in a clergyman..
Now, Rose! - You'll be givin' Ruby 'ere ideas! Wot's 'is name, anyway?
Um.. some fancy French fing.. Oo! Nearly forgot! - 'E said to give you this...
Bishop.. erm... Michelin! - That's 'im!
Rose!!
Michelin Good Food Guide

You may think that the name 'Christine de Pizan' has a rather un-British ring about it. Right first time! She isn't one of Ours, worse luck: born in Venice, she spent most of her life in France, shaking up the courts of Charles V and VI. So, what's she doing in an insular book like this? Well, the short answer is that she was a stunner – a real live literate feminist who argued women's corner with cogency, spirit, elegance and persistence.

Is it depressing or cheering to discover that as early as 1405 a woman writer was describing, dissecting and protesting against the long history of oppression suffered by women? Well, you'll have to make up your own minds about that. But snarls and the gnashing of teeth surely cannot be avoided over the fact that this writer's words were allowed to drop into a black hole for several centuries. Like so many other women of achievement, she just Got Lost. One of the major works of Christine de Pizan – *The Book of the City of Ladies* – was newly translated into English in 1982. It had last been translated in 1521, which may strike you as being a long time even for the slow mills of publishing.

Married at the age of 15 (not uncommon in those days), Christine de Pizan was a widow by the time she was 25. She also had three children, no inherited money, an excellent education (thanks to her father's unusual views on the suitable upbringing for a female child) and vividly happy memories of a supportive and much-loved husband. Using her connections at Charles V's court – her father had been Astrologer By Appointment – Christine set out to make her living by writing.

Although she was probably the first woman to become a professional writer, her distinction lies far beyond any such entry in a book of records. Between 1390 and 1429, Christine de Pizan produced an array of works in both verse and prose, commanding widespread admiration for her literary versatility and her intellectual powers. Recognised as an accomplished lyric poet, she also served as the official biographer of Charles V. But her professional success and her literary stature never prevented her from entering into controversy. The two main themes which ran through her work were the appeal for peace (the France of her day was a bloody and divided kingdom) and the demand that women should be fully recognised as valuable human beings and citizens.

An erudite woman of high Christian principle, Christine de Pizan honed her arguments in order to defeat her male opponents on their own ground as well as to open up new fields of debate. *The Romance of the Rose,* a central work of medieval French literature and one which embodied the strange contradictions of the theory of courtly love, she judged to be immoral in general and misogynistic in particular. Accordingly, she joined forces with some other (male) intellectuals and launched a stinging attack both on the work and on the mind-set which had produced it. Known – magnificently – as the Quarrel of *The Romance of the Rose,* this attack raised the European cultural rafters.

She pursued her feminist theme in many other works, including a long poem in honour of Joan of Arc (the only literary praise which Joan received during her lifetime). In two books of prose – *The Book of the City of Ladies* and the *Livre des Trois Vertus* – Christine de Pizan gave extraordinarily vivid and cogent expression to her views on women's state. An allegory, *The Book of the City of Ladies* represents the creation of a secure place for women – a place where their feats are recognised, their memories revered and their future given new hope.

The narrative calls on the life of Medea (an ace herbalist, Christine points out approvingly), the Roman Empress Triaria, the Virgin Mary, and most stations in between. The accounts of different women's lives are intercut with sharp refutations of common slanders against women. Listen, for example, to what the allegorical figure, Lady Rectitude, has to say about the meaning of marriage for many women:

> How many women are there actually, dear friend – and you yourself know – who because of their husbands' harshness spend their weary lives in the bond of marriage in greater suffering than if they were slaves among the Saracens! My God! How many harsh beatings – without cause and without reason – how many injuries, how many cruelties, insults, humiliations, and outrages have so many upright women suffered, none of whom cried out for help? And consider all the women who die of hunger and grief with a home full of children, while their husbands carouse dissolutely or go on binges in every tavern all over town, and still the poor women are beaten by their husbands when they return, and *that* is their supper!

Lady R. later addresses the question of whether women are naturally greedy:

> Women are usually kept in such financial straits that they guard the little that they can have, knowing they can recover this only with the greatest pain. So some people consider women greedy because some women have foolish husbands, great wastrels of property and gluttons, and the poor women, who know well that their households need what their husbands spend foolishly and that in the end the poor children will have to pay for it, are unable to refrain from speaking to their husbands and from urging them to spend less. Thus, such behaviour is not at all avarice or greed, but is a sign of great prudence.

At another point, after describing several examples of the constancy and depth of women's love, Rectitude adds a tart reminder.

> But these pitiful examples, as well as many others which I could also tell you, should in no way move women's hearts to set themselves adrift in the dangerous and damnable sea of foolish love, for its end is always detrimental and harmful to their bodies, their property, their honor, and – most important of all – to their souls. Women should conduct themselves wisely and with good sense and should know how to avoid this kind of love and not to listen to those who incessantly strive to deceive them in such cases.

It's over 500 years since all those words were written. How much more time do we need?

Maggie Smith
Theatre
Julia McKenzie
Mona Washbourne · Maureen Lipman · Liz Smith · Julie Walters
Elizabeth Spriggs · Billie Whitelaw · Gwen Watford
Dame Margaret Rutherford 1892 - 1972
Mrs. Patrick Campbell 1865 - 1940
Sarah Siddons 1755 - 1831
Dame Edith Evans 1888 - 1976
Dame Ellen Terry 1847 - 1928
Joyce Grenfell 1910 - 1979
Nell Gwynne 1650 - 1687
Dame Peggy Ashcroft b. 1907
Dame Celia Johnson 1908 - 1982
Rachel Roberts 1927 - 1980
Beryl Reid b. 1920
Gertrude Lawrence 1898 - 1952
Dame Marie Tempest 1864 - 1942
Kitty Clive 1711 - 1785
Dame Sybil Thorndike 1882 - 1976
Siân Phillips
Diana Rigg b. 1938
Frances de la Tour b. 1944
Sheila Hancock Actor & Director
Judi Dench b. 1934
Vanessa Redgrave b. 1937
Cathleen Nesbitt 1882 - 1982
Anne Oldfield 1683 - 1730
Miriam Margolyes
Dame Flora Robson b. 1902 - d. 1984
Vivien Leigh 1913 - 1967
Glenda Jackson b. 1936
Peg Woffington c. 1714 - 1760
Miriam Karlin
Dandy Nichols d. 1986

ALL THAT..
5. Unclean Acts
DOWN THERE
SEX WAS AN UNCLEAN ACT. PEOPLE STANK... RICH & POOR REEKED. DISEASE, FILTH & HALITOSIS MAY NOT HAVE PUT PEOPLE OFF, BUT THEY MIGHT HAVE MADE ONE OR TWO THINK TWICE..
GASP!
it's not like this in books...
ONE DAY (HAVING TAKEN OVER HAIR-COMBING DUTIES) MRS. PEPYS FOUND 20 LICE IN HER HUSBAND'S HAIR..
well... it is only Tuesday..
INDEED, HE HARDLY WASHED HIS BODY UNTIL 1664, WHEN SHE FLEETINGLY DISCOVERED THE DELIGHTS OF HOT WATER - NOT LETTING HIM ANYWHERE NEAR TILL HE WASHED. PEPYS GAVE IN, AFTER 3 DAYS..
oof
IN 1700, AT CHATSWORTH, THE DUKE OF BEDFORD HAD A BATHROOM INSTALLED.. BUT THIS WAS AN EXCEPTION...
THE FRENCH INVENTED BIDETS - BUT THE ENGLISH DISAPPROVED ON MORAL GROUNDS...
a foote-bathe?!
POOR WOMEN WORE IRON OR WHALEBONE-STIFFENED STAYS FOR DECADES WITHOUT CLEANING.. PADDED PETTICOATS WERE WORN UNTIL THEY DISINTEGRATED...
h'mm.. time for a new one...
PING
PAFF!
CHEAP COTTON CLOTHES & SOAP, & MORE WASHING FACILITIES, ONLY ARRIVED IN THE 19TH CENTURY - & NOT BEFORE TIME..
s'great! You wear one while you wash the other!
- & MY MUM REMEBERS LITTLE GIRLS, GREASED & SEWN INTO THEIR UNDERWEAR FOR THE WINTER.. (Barnsley Road Junior, Wombwell Yorks c.1932)
they do leave a hole, miss..

Jobs for Women
Well, I was really into Architecture.
7 · Nun
Jobs for Women
I thought of calling myself a therapist but it lacks the right amount of awe...
yeah...
8 · Wise Woman
Jobs for Women
Been at the Rhubarb again, eh?
CLENCH
9 · Herbalist

MODULE 6

Which Witch?

If you happened to be born female in the fifteenth, sixteenth or seventeenth centuries and grew up to be poor, stubborn, proud and sharp-tongued, your opportunities for self-fulfilment were, frankly, rather limited. You couldn't go on television. You couldn't get involved in the women's movement. You couldn't even get into middle management. How *could* you get people to take you seriously?

That was a rhetorical question, folks. Please put your pens – and hands – down even if you think you know the right answer. We've never come across such a rush for gold stars, never, in all our years of....

At this point we're going to bow to pressure from within and without and introduce a guest speaker. Witchcraft (yes, well *done*!) is such a misunderstood profession that we thought it only right to allow a representative from the British College of Witchcraft to put the practitioner's point of view. Stepping across the centuries, we offer access to the thoughts of the progressive witch of the seventeenth century. Afterwards, we'll attempt to bore you stiff by introducing some *balance* into the discussion.

QUIZ

If your neighbour accused you of having an unconventional relationship both with your cat and the Prince of Darkness, would you be inclined to:

(a) report her goings-on to a DHSS super snooper?
(b) suggest deep Jungian analysis?
(c) confess all?
(d) explain that you are a lesbian and so interested only in the cat?
(e) conduct a balanced discussion with her on the sociological/anthropological context of Europe's witch-hunts?

Hmm ... perhaps you should think about moving house before something awkward happens.

Anyway, please now give a warm welcome to our guest from the British College of Witchcraft.

THE BRITISH COLLEGE OF
WITCHCRAFT
Information Sheet
Thirty Firft October 1660.
Broomftick? Cat? It's all Old Hat!
HAVE YOU GOT WHAT IT TAKES FOR WITCHCRAFT TODAY?
Times are Changing!
No longer do recruits to WITCHCRAFT need to feel embaraffed by their Calling. To-day's Witch is acknowledged to be in Poffeffion of State-of-the-Art Knowledge as:
PHYSICIAN PHARMACIST COUNSELLOR
MIDWIFE ANATOMIST HEALER
Not An Eafy Life!
The Life ifn't an eafy one, & a succesfful Career in Witchcraft demands Application, Discretion & Ingenuity. *NB The College does not Recognife Prowefs in the Black Arts. * Recognifed Witches take an Uncompromifing Quality of Life Stand.
But A Rewarding One!
But for Thofe (in England & Wales) who Develop their Talent for Healing - the Rewards are High!*
Once You are Known in Your Community as a Cunning Woman, You can play a Full Part in extending the National Health Service to thofe in moft need.
You Will Alfo Gain
RESPECT FAME GIFTS of EGGS, CHICKENS &tc
THE OPPORTUNITY to TRAVEL
Afpiring WITCHES are Reminded that the College confiders it Highly Unethical - & Dangerous - to Advertife their Profeffional Services.
BUT!
BE POSITIVE! THINK 'WORD-of-MOUTH'
& PARALYSE the MAN-MIDWIFE Competition!!
*Applications from SCOTLAND cannot be considered, as the Scottish Authorities still make NO distinction between Healer & Curser. Most Witches convicted in Scotland are strangled & burned.

Well, thanks, sisters. I wonder what they would make of this peculiar rash on my shin? Rude to ask, I suppose ... Oh, sorry, didn't realise you lot were back already. Hope you found all that interesting and useful. What do you mean, you thought you were listening to an SDP broadcast? Oh, you extremists are all the same ...

Yes, all right, now for the Balance. The Balance is that if you had no intention of helping anyone, you could become a Witch witch and have a helluva time scaring the knickers off your neighbours. In 1667, for example, Issobel Grierson was alleged to have said to a fellow Scot, 'The faggotis of hell lycht on the, and hellis caldrane may thow seith in'; while Agnes Finnie of Potterrow in Edinburgh, accused of witchcraft in 1642, had allegedly commented that, 'she should gar the Devil take a bite of the said Bessie Currie'. Elizabeth Bathgate is reputed to have told her victim, George Sprot, 'for work what you can your teeth shall overgang your hands and ye shall never get your Sundays meat to the fore'. Madeleine Blair commented in her confession that, 'she never gave a malison [curse] but what shee saw light'.

Fine stuff – but, as we have seen, the penalties, especially in Scotland, were horrendous. And most confessions were extracted during torture. The words of the witches may or may not have hurt their victims; they certainly hurt the witches themselves.

Why did women become 'wicked' witches? Well, some didn't – but were executed all the same, poor, uneducated, powerless to save themselves. Others perhaps saw in this craft one way out of the poverty trap. Where respect was lacking, fear could provide an effective substitute. And then there were the promises made by the Devil. More frequently than their English sisters, Scottish witches were expected to enter into a Demonic Pact, which ensured that their immortal souls were sold at the market rate. For Bessie Wilson, this meant being told that, 'thee art a poor puddled [overworked] body. Will thee be my servant and I will give thee abundance and thee shall never want'. Another novice was told that she would have 'all the pleasure of the earth'.

More frequently, however, the rewards came in the form of the food served at the Witches' Sabbaths. Oatcakes and ale was said to be the standard fare for such occasions; but if you got in with a good crowd, you could expect wine, wheaten cake and meat.

ACTIVITY

Jot down a few good reasons why the souls of poor Scottish women should be worth so much less than that of the eminent Dr Faustus.

English women, however, didn't have it that much better. In 1645, on her way to Westleton, Elizabeth Southern met the Devil. He promised her 2/6d, but then failed to let her have it, complaining 'of the hardness of the times'.

The damage put down to witches was known as *maleficium.* This nasty-sounding activity could take a variety of forms, including:

- causing injury or death to other people
- killing or injuring farm animals
- interfering with nature by, say, preventing a cow from giving milk
- frustrating domestic operations such as the making of butter, cheese or milk
- interfering with the weather – for example, storm-raising (a Scottish speciality, can't think why)

It was this maleficium that got the neighbours dancing their rage in the streets; but by the late Middle Ages, Church and State had agreed that such goings-on were of secondary importance. The real crime was the heresy of Devil-worship. The woman convicted of being a witch deserved to die not for flattening crops or for destroying livestock but for being an enemy of God: hers was a 'thought' crime.

Self-check question

Think of your own last 'thought' crime. If you'd know then what you know now about the different varieties of maleficium, how might you have developed your thought into action?

Writers 1
Iris Murdoch
Muriel Spark
Dilys Powell
Mrs. Thrale
Edith Somerville & Violet Martin (Ross)
Alice Meynell
Daphne du Maurier
Sue Townsend
Dorothy Wordsworth
Stella Gibbons
Mary Shelley
Jessica Mitford
Dame Rebecca West. b. 1892 - d. 1983
Vita Sackville-West 1892 - 1962
1806-61 Elizabeth Barratt Browning
Virginia Woolf 1882-1941
Antonia White 1899-1980
Richmal Crompton
Jean Rhys 1894-1979
Kathleen Raine. Poet b. 1908
Nancy Spain Journalist. 1917-1964
Naomi Mitchison b. 1897
Dame Edith Sitwell 1887-1964
Radclyffe Hall 1883-1943
Beryl Bainbridge b. 1934
Margery Allingham. 1904-1966
Anne · Emily · Charlotte Brontë 1820-49, 1818-48, 1816-55
Christina Rossetti. Poet 1830-1894
Dorothy L. Sayers 1893-1958
Mrs. Gaskell 1810-1865
Sue Arnold Journalist.
Catherine Philips 1631-1664
Elizabeth Taylor. 1912-1975
Ivy Compton-Burnett. 1892-1969
Rosamund Lehmann b. 1903
Elizabeth Bowen 1899-1973
Stevie Smith 1902-1971
Angela Carter
Olivia Manning

MODULE 7

The Askit Letters: the secret correspondence of Mary and Elizabeth

Two queens in a kingdom! Many a wise greybeard (and the sales of Grecian 2000 were up, up, up in those days) stroked their fronds nervously as they contemplated the competing claims of Elizabeth Tudor and Mary Stuart. Who deserved the Throne of England? Was it the daughter of Henry VIII and Anne Boleyn – that determined young woman whom many called illegitimate and many others called bastard? Or was it Mary Stuart, daughter of James V of Scotland and somebody else, who had yet another complicated reason for thinking that she should be IT?

We won't give the story away – merely point you in the direction of some recently discovered correspondence between the two queens – Elizabeth, Acting Queen of England and Mary, Queen of Scots.

Many of you will be familiar with the Casket Letters (we can't say we've browsed through them ourselves). This collection seems to have been used as general evidence against poor old Mary – though why she should be frowned on for writing to a casket, we can't tell. The following sequence is rapidly becoming known as The Askit Letters since they would give any scholar a headache.

ACTIVITY

Do not discover that your plants need watering. Read the letters. Then answer the self-check questions at the end. *Then* water the plants.

London
November, 1560

Mary Stuart
Ex-Dauphiness
France

My dear Cousin
Yes, of course I'm sorry that your young husband has died, even though he was French and a Catholic. But, no, I wouldn't recommend Scotland at this time of year – or indeed at any other. It's not just the weather – though, incidentally, my spies tell me that it's particularly hellish this year. (Whoops! Swearbox! Blame your namesake, my half-sister, Mary. No wonder people called her Bloody Mary.) The *general climate*, my dear, is not very favourable towards a nice Catholic girl like yourself. There's a craze, I understand, for men in black to stand up in bare churches and screech insults and threats against all present. DV, I can stop anything like *that* happening down south!

Dear old Dad would have *boomed* at the idea that's just come to me. 'You want to hear a good Catholic joke?' people used to say, 'then just whisper "Papal Bull" to Henry VIII.' But I digress. What I wondered was – have you thought about going into a nunnery?
Yours ever

PS I've just heard that the exchange rate between France and Ecosse is *way down*.

Edinburgh
September, 1561

Elizabeth Regina
London

My dear Coz
Well, here I am, safe and sound, you'll be glad to hear! I can't say the journey was up to much: it would have made life easier if your Government could have granted me a passport to travel through England. But, there, I know how awkward bureaucrats can be; you did your best, I'm sure.

I'm touched by your suggestion that I marry Robert Dudley, Earl of Leicester, since I know how fond you are of him. (Amazing, isn't it, how news travels? I heard a marvellous ballad only yesterday about how you discovered that he was the best candidate for the post of Master of Horse.) Funny old business about his wife, wasn't it? Poor woman, falling down the stairs and breaking her neck like that. You must both have been terribly upset.

Anyway, dear Coz, I feel that Dudley's perhaps a *wee* bit common for me; I had been looking at the market in terms of a premium, blue-blooded product, like a powerful European prince (Catholic, of course!). But I *might* be persuaded to give the Master Horseman a few more points if you were to reveal publicly your intention of making me your heir. Just a formality, of course, since we both know that I've got just as much right to the throne of England as you have! Funny old world, eh?
Yours ever

Marie

PS Is it true that you've got a real *dish* at *your* court – a cousin of mine, Henry Darnley? The men are so *rough* up here.

London
August, 1565

Mary Stuart
Edinburgh

Dear Cousin
Of course, you must have been disappointed that Robert Dudley didn't want to marry you – but you really shouldn't have abducted Henry Darnley. For your own good, I have to tell you that everybody at *this* court thinks he's a right wimp. And there are *habits*, I understand. I hope you don't live to regret this hasty marriage.

Don't worry: I have no intention of splicing any knots myself. The family background really puts one off. Frankly, would *you* want to get married if your father had had six wives and had knocked your mother's block off? On the other hand, I see no reason for rushing into the heir-naming business. And if it comes to it, dear, who knows – I may outlive you yet.

By the way, I found your emissary, Sir James Melville, positively charming. Just fancy, he commented that he had never heard *any* queen play better on the virginals! (And if your court's the same as mine, that's really saying something!)
Yours ever

Dunbar
April, 1566

The so-called Queen of England & Ireland
(just a joke!)

Dear Cousin
If it's not one thing, it's another! No sooner had I chased Moray and his fellow-Protestant rebels out of the country – what have they got against dear Henry anyway? – than *another* lot turned on me in my own home! (I wish you could see Holyrood – I've got it very cosy.) *Quel pays!*

Anyway, musical evenings will never be the same again because my poor David Rizzio has had his last ice-cream cone. In the sinister mutter that so many Scots employ, it's been hinted to me that Henry might have had something to do with the murderous attack. But, *entre nous*, he is indeed on the wimpish side and I doubt that he would have been up to much plotting. I never knew a man so plagued by headaches.

As you know, I'm about to be lighter of a fair son (cross fingers!). In my condition, I must say I could do without having to scheme to regain control of the wretched country. Wish me luck for a safe return to Edinburgh.

Slainte mhath

Mhairi

Somewhere on a Progress
July, 1566

The Queen of Scots

Dear Mary

I'm so glad that you've avoided all the many potentially lethal perils attendant on childbirth these days.

How nice! A boy! What a thrill for me, being but a barren stock myself.

Yes, I'll be godmother. How kind of you to ask.

A splendid silver-gilt font follows under separate cover.

Yours

Holyrood
February, 1567

Elizabeth Regina
England

Dear Bess
Just think what's happened now! Henry's been blown up! I knew I should have nationalised gas.

I fear that some ugly rumours may reach your ears regarding the regrettable accident. It may be hinted that in the company of my Lord Bothwell and sundry others (names supplied) I did conspire to bring about the tragic death of my husband, the father of my son. Well, I trust that *you* know how much weight to attach to such vile insinuations!

I'm overwhelmed by grief.

Such a fun night last Thursday – a ceilidh for the Highland chieftains. And I can't *wait* for Saturday night – Bothwell says he'll sing me some of these old Border Ballads. Quaint!

Yours aye

The Throne of England
May, 1567

MQS (cipher)

Cousin!
What is this I hear? That, having ignored my right royal advice *re* making a decent pretence of grief over your (second) husband's death, you have now allowed yourself to be abducted – and married! – by that tinker Bothwell? That you held a 'show trial' (new buzz word here) of Bothwell at which Lennox, the prosecutor, was afraid to appear since he was allowed only 6 followers against the 4,000 granted to Bothwell?

Dear old Dad might have thought all that kind of thing hunky-dory; but, frankly, I think you want your *head examined.*

Pull your royal garters up, my girl!

Yours

TO: ER COMMA LONDON — EDINBURGH JUNE 1567

OH GAWD EXCLAMATION MARK UPRISINGS HAVE UPROOTED ME STOP BOTHWELL FLED THE FIELD DASH RAT STOP IMPRISONED IN EDINBURGH STOP POPULACE WANT MY ROYAL GUTS FOR GARTERS STOP CAN I COME TO ENGLAND QUESTION MARK MQS

TO: MQS COMMA EDINBURGH — LONDON JUNE 1567

HORRIFIED TO GET YOUR TELEGRAM STOP WHAT A BLOODY MESS EXCLAMATION MARK NO COMMA YOU CANT COME HERE STOP ACCOMMODATION BEING ARRANGED FOR YOU IN LOCHLEVEN CASTLE STOP RECOMMEND SIGN ABDICATION FORM DASH IN TRIPLICATE STOP ER

Carlisle
May, 1568

ER
London

Gloriana!
Well, here I am at last! Fife, my dear, was Dullsville so I escaped p.d.q. But – isn't it awful? – I don't have a *thing* to wear, so, before you invite me to court, I'd much appreciate your sending me a few rags.
How soon do you think your armies will get over the Border and crush this ridiculous rebellion?
Never say die!

Westminster
June, 1568

MQS
Carlisle

Dear Cousin
I'm glad that you're safe.
Welcome to England.
I'm sending Sir Francis Knollys to take charge of your establishment. He will give you some garments.
Yours

Carlisle
July, 1568

ER
London

Dear Cousin
I know I said 'a few rags', but really! On opening your parcel, I found:
ITEM Two worn-out chemises
ITEM A length of black velvet
ITEM A pair of shoes (wrong size)
Your English sense of humour, I suppose! I can see that I've got a lot to learn!
Ha-ha

PS Sir F. (sweet man!) has told me that you've a *thing* about clothes, dating back to your unhappy childhood. You can't bear to part with anything nice! Poor thing! Sometimes, you know, it can help just to lie back on a couch and talk away to a man with a beard and a foreign accent. Have a reccy among the Ambassadors, why don't you? There's bound to be one to fit the bill.

The sequence of letters now falters. Only four remain – two exchanges, separated by a period of some years.

Westminster
June, 1570

MQS
Tetbury Castle, Staffs.

Dear Mary
Stop plotting!
Yours ever

Tetbury Castle
Staffs
July 1570

ER
London

Dear Elizabeth
Get me out of here!
Yours

Mary

Westminster
April 1582

MQS
Tetbury Castle, Staffs.

Dear Mary
Stop plotting!
Yours

Chartley
Staffs.
May 1582

ER
London

Dear Elizabeth
Get me out of here!
Yours

Mary

Self-check questions

1 In your opinion, what kind of factors might have persuaded Mary Stuart to marry a French dolphin? Would one have expected the dolphin to be Catholic or Protestant? (If your preferred answer is C of E, you should now consider taking an emergency break to water the plants.)

2 If, in June, 1568, Elizabeth had sent Mary a pair of shoes of the right size, in your opinion would Mary have continued to plot against her?

3 After gazing for some moments at the portraits of the period scattered over your walls, write a paragraph outlining why you think that Elizabeth and Mary may have had legs.

MODULE 8

Speaking Out: pamphleteers, prophetesses and actresses

Considerable male effort has been expended over the years on attempting to persuade women that

(a) we have nothing to say because we're stupid

and

(b) if we have something to say that, by some miracle, isn't stupid, then we shouldn't say it anyway because it's more than likely to be wicked.

By 'over the years' we mean, of course, the Middle Ages, the Renaissance, the seventeenth century, the eighteenth century and all other stations on the line.

During the sixteenth and seventeenth centuries, pamphlets provided a popular means of nailing the stupid/wicked/*treacherous* creatures. Joseph Swetnam, for example, got up a fine head of steam in 1617 when in his *Arraignment of Lewd, Idle, Froward and Unconstant Women* he commented that:

> Many women are in shape angels but in qualities devils, painted coffins with rotten bones.... Although women are beautiful, showing pity, yet their hearts are black, swelling with mischief, not much unlike unto old trees whose outward leaves are fair and green and yet the body rotten.

Several painted coffins with rotten bones were unwilling to let such stuff pass unchallenged. In her reply to Swetnam, *A Muzzle for Melastromus*, Rachel Speght, the young daughter of a clergyman, delivered a full frontal attack designed to hit both Swetnam and his arguments where it hurt most. Soaring down from lofty scriptural refutation of his cant, she seizes him by the literary jugular:

> (Page 11, line 8.) You count it 'wonderful to see the mad feats of women, for she will now be merry, then sad'. But methinks it is far more *wonder-fool* to have one that adventures to make his writing as public as an inn-keeper's sign, which hangs to the view of all passengers, to want grammatical concordance in his said writing: and join together 'women' plural and 'she' singular, *ass* you not only in this place but also in others have done.

Self-check question Can you begin to see why men might have wanted women to keep silent?

Rachel Speght was not alone in her desire for revenge. Several other women composed stinging replies to Swetnam's pamphlet; and in 1619 the Red Bull theatre reverberated with a new hit play: *Swetnam the Woman-Hater arraigned by Women.* Don't ask about the main plot, but the sub-plot has S the W-H getting duffed up by a load of unruly and jolly cross female persons (or painted coffins).

Early Vigilante Patrol

However, despite such spirited responses, History being what he is, Swetnam's words, and not the women's, were to be reprinted regularly over the next hundred years.

Even before Swetnam set himself up as a baiter of women, the voice of an Englishwoman had been heard defending her sex against male slander. An early (1589) pamphlet under the name of Jane Anger set a newly bracing pace for a girl-to-girl chat:

> Fie on the falsehood of men, whose minds go oft a-madding and whose tongues cannot so soon be wagging, but straight they fall a-tattling! Was there ever any so abused, so slandered, so railed upon, or so wickedly handled undeservedly, as are we women? Will the gods permit it, the goddesses stay their punishing judgements, and we ourselves not pursue their undoings for such devilish practices? O Paul's steeple and Charing Cross! A halter hold all such persons. Let the streams of the channels in London streets run so swiftly as they may be able alone to carry them from that sanctuary. Let the stones be as ice, the soles of their shoes as glass, the ways steep like Etna, and every blast a whirlwind puffed out of Boreas his long throat, that these may hasten their passage to the devil's haven.

The author goes on to counter men's charges against women (treachery, wickedness, lustfulness). She also points out that the male notion of 'love', both theory and practice, itself offers not a few pitfalls to women. For example:

> The smooth speeches of men are nothing unlike the vanishing clouds of the air, which glide by degrees from place to place till they have filled themselves with rain, when, breaking, they spit forth terrible showers. So men gloze till they have their answers, which are the end of their travail, and then they bid modesty adieu and, entertaining rage, fall a-railing on us which never hurt them.

ACTIVITY

Who do you think might know what 'gloze' means? Phone them up and ask them.

A woman refusing to Compromise her Integrity

The woman pamphleteers were brave – and probably lucky – exceptions. For a start, they had somehow or other acquired considerable education, thus overcoming odds not unsimilar to the snowball's chance of remaining cold and cheery in hell. For another thing, they had achieved access to the printed word – the kind of printed word, moreover, which found comparatively wide circulation. In times when women seem to have been criticised for even talking to their husbands, these writers scored double marks – for speaking in public and for defending their sex.

Despite their lack of education and despite the taboos on women's utterances, many other women too felt the need to find a public voice. Witchcraft, as we have seen, offered one career path; but one apt to be blocked by extremely large boulders. Another option lay on the right side of the spiritual blanket, so to speak. If, as the Puritans asserted, men and women were equal in the eyes of God, then surely women had the right – nay, the *duty* – to speak out when the Spirit moved them?

And, by God, they did. There was the additional advantage, of course, that if your knowledge and words came from the highest source, then you could afford to look somewhat contemptuously on the world of secondary sources denied to you. Thus, Anna Trapnel, a prophetess associated with the (surely inspired) Fifth Monarchist movement, made clear the limitations of tertiary education:

> Thou shalt not read what's spoke of Dragon and Beast
> With University-art;
> But thou shalt read with Kings seven eyes
> And an enlightened heart.
>
> Thou shalt not run to Antichrists Libraries
> To fetch from thence any skill
> To read the Revelation of Christ,
> But be with knowledge fill'd.

Like many other prophetesses and 'She preachers', Anna Trapnel found her finest hour between 1640 and 1654 when Cromwell's Government proved deliciously susceptible to ecstatic visions. Stern senior executive Roundheads interrupted their councils on several occasions to hearken to the message of the Almighty as transmitted through His humble female servants.

Self-check question

Can you feel a vision welling up? What would you most like to tell the Prime Minister and her Cabinet?

However, things were considered by the boardroom to be getting a bit out of hand when the extremist Fifth Monarchists started to identify Cromwell, the Lord Protector, with the 'Little Horn', a revolting Apocryphal excrescence; the Army, similarly, once known as the Army of Saints, assumed a perhaps more interesting new persona as the Army of the Beast. It was hard for them though to argue with the voice of God, and many a prophetess, including Anna Trapnel, must have gloried in the inability of those in authority to shut her up.

ACTIVITY

In the illustration below, what do you think the prophetess is saying to Cromwell and his merry men? Write in the space provided.

Not that the work was easy. Fasting, sleeplessness and trances were all required to keep ecstatic prophecies up to the mark. You also had to make sure that no one important thought you were a witch. After all, inspired and talkative women were more than likely to be up to no good and, if God *wasn't* on your side, you could be sure as hell that no one else would be either.

The ability to prophesy seems to have cut across class lines. At one extreme, Lady Eleanor Davies pursued a spectacular career which included foretelling the execution of Charles I (much to his annoyance) and the assassination of the Duke of Buckingham.

At the other, Jane Hawkins, 'a poor woman (and she but a pedlar)', achieved considerable fame in Huntingdon in 1629 when she was seized with a fit of prophetic rhyming which lasted three days and nights. Perhaps rashly, God included in the script advance notice that all bishops were to be made redundant; the local Bish took this news in a less than Christian spirit and handed the unfortunate woman over to the Justices of the Peace.

In the 1640s, 'She preachers' (offering letters rather than telegrams from God) got a foothold in some English churches. Others preached to congregations in their own homes – though it must be said that some of these could have done with footstools as well as footholds. A certain Mary Bilbrowe, wife of a bricklayer of St Giles-in-the-Fields, preached in her parlour from a brick pulpit so high that only her tippet could be seen.

ACTIVITY

Having adapted your sitting-room to accommodate a brick pulpit, decide which tippet you would most like to be seen in.

'She preachers', like prophetesses, aroused a great deal of male unease and criticism. Not only did they on occasion raise awkward issues of social injustice but they also flourished the inflammable banner of 'freedom of conscience'. And once *that* was extended to women, where might it all end? If a woman had the right to choose in one sphere, mightn't she begin to look askance at compulsion in other areas? What about the husband's rights in marriage, for example? Or, for that matter, the institution of marriage itself?

Such fears were partly justified, we're delighted to report. While this particular wave of prophetesses died away after the 1660s, their banners were lifted again in the eighteenth century, when several women, including Ann Lee and Joanna Southcott, promised a new life to the poor and dispossessed. Ann Lee saw celibacy as the necessary prelude to spiritual liberation; while Joanna Southcott believed that she would give birth to the second saviour of the world (the pregnancy proved to be 'hysterical'). To these female voices, as to others of radical, if strange, vision, many women listened intently and responded with passion.

Prophetesses and female preachers were not, of course, the only women to speak out loud from a pre-ordained script. The Restoration of Charles II in 1660 heralded both the re-opening of the theatres (dark for 18 years while those illumined by the Lord ran the land) and the introduction of 'actoresses'.

What a blow for the boys! Gone were all those lovely parts where they could wear frocks as well as breeches, swoon, sigh and generally camp it up rotten. Now it was the women's turn to swagger – no doubt with equal glee – into the 'breeches' parts of the old plays (you know, Shakespeare and all that) and the astoundingly earthy roles offered by the new ones (Behn, Wycherley, Congreve, and so on).

Self-check question

Be honest – which Shakespearean 'breeches' part have you always yearned after? *Why* do you think Viola has the edge over Rosalind?

Job opportunities being otherwise somewhat limited, young women flocked in droves to London's stages. Some had been brought up gently and had acquired the ladylike skills of singing and dancing without the dowry necessary to underwrite these talents in the marriage market. Others had been drug up any old how and were quite happy to learn the singing and dancing bit if they could count on there being a fair number of lecherous and rich men in their audiences. (They could.) Yet others came from theatrical families and already knew the score. The wonder is that this motley crew was acknow-

ledged to have achieved and maintained a generally high standard of acting within a very short space of time.

The earliest professional actresses to achieve prominence were Mary Saunderson (later Betterton) and Anne Marshall (later Quin), of the rival Duke's Company and King's Company respectively. The first was noted for her virtue as well as her talent (the former quality seeming particularly remarkable to many observers). The second proved well cut out for the new 'heroic drama' à la Dryden as well as for inter-familial feud. When her talented younger sister, Rebecca, looked set to usurp all her big roles, Anne Marshall immediately petitioned the Lord Chamberlain for redress. The result was that in 1667 the King's Company was instructed to admit the aggrieved star 'to Act again at Theatre Royall and that you assign her all her own parts which she formerly had and that none other be permitted to act any of her parts without her consent. And that you assign her a dressing room with a chimney in it to be only for her use and whom she shall admit'.

How the words 'So *there*!' came to be omitted from the instruction, we're at a loss to explain.

ACTIVITY

Write a song entitled, 'Sisters, sisters'.

In the highly charged world of the theatre, it wasn't only sisters who irritated the hell out of each other. The splendid Elizabeth Barry, queen of the boards from the 1670s until 1710, reached her sticking point during a pre-performance quarrel with her fellow leading lady, Mrs Boutel. (The play was entitled 'The Rival Queens'; the quarrel was over a scarf – what else?) In true professional style, the show went on; but the line

Die, sorceress, die and all my wrongs die with thee!

proved too much for the still-inflamed Mrs Barry and she seized the opportunity to employ her blunt stage dagger to better effect than was ever intended by the playwright. Mrs Boutel's stays, we regret to say, were pierced.

However, such excitements apart, a good deal of cameraderie and solidarity existed amongst the actresses (and the one noted female playwright, Aphra Behn). They had quite a lot to develop solidarity about. The money was awful. Young actresses would be expected to work for nothing at the start of their careers; after gaining some experience, they would be awarded 10s. to 15s. a week (not a lot). Even the top rates (30s. to 50s. a week) didn't go far towards keeping leading ladies in the style to which they were expected to become accustomed.

As a result, many distinguished actresses (not to mention a good few other undistinguished ones) did some moonlighting as mistresses to wealthy men. From the men's point of view, an important matter of status was at stake. No one who was *anyone* (and *everyone* went to the theatre) could admit failure to be on uncommonly familiar terms with at least one of the women on stage.

Self-check question

What other little games do you think the gentlemen may have played amongst themselves?

Sometimes, though, it was a question of even stronger feelings. The Earl of Oxford fell so heavily for a well-known actress, Hester Davenport, that in his distraction (his feelings were unreciprocated) he could neither smoke nor gamble. Obviously, such a drastic condition could not be allowed to continue, and Lord Oxford, Knight of the Garter, took the heroic course of pretending to marry the actress. When, next morning, Hester Davenport was woken by her 'husband's' instruction that it was time for her to go, she realised that she had been betrayed and – some of you may be glad to hear – delivered him a stinging wound with his own sword.

Nell Gwynn, an excellent comedy actress, did better in many ways with her protector, Charles II. Brought up in a bawdy house with a boozer for a mother and a father dead in a debtors' prison, she graduated from raking ashes and selling apples and herrings to selling oranges at the Theatre Royal (many a young girl's path to relative prosperity). Somehow or other, she learned to read and write; and also inveigled the actors of the King's Company into giving her lessons in the dramatic arts. Her talent was spotted ('My God, surely *that's* not the little girl who . . .') and she made her stage debut in 1664, soon establishing a popular following. One of her first lovers was a fellow actor, Charles Hart; she then moved on to a friend of the King, Lord Charles Buckhurst. When, in 1667, she got together with the King himself, she referred to him, logically enough, as her Charles III. Shrewd, good-tempered and very funny, Nell Gwynn made a considerable success of both her careers.

Actors are unlucky in that they can be appreciated only at a blurred distance by later generations. However, despite the ribaldries and the rivalries, it's clear that the advent of women to the English stage opened many eyes to an immensely widened range of dramatic possibilities. Attention was often serious and respectful; sometimes, it was awed. Listen, for example, to what the actor, Colley Cibber, had to say about the grande dame, Elizabeth Barry:

> Mrs Barry, in Characters of Greatness, had a Presence of elevated Dignity, her Mien and Motion superb and gracefully majestick; her Voice full, clear, and strong, so that no Violence of Passion could be too much for her: and When Distress or Tenderness possess'd her, she subsided into the most affecting Melody and Softness. In the Art of exciting Pity She had a Power beyond all the Actresses I have yet seen, or what your Imagination can conceive.

WOMAN · OF · THE · AGE
OROONOKO
1640 · APHRA · BEHN · 1689

> What has poor woman done that she must be
> Debarr'd from sense, and sacred poetry?
> Why in this age has Heaven allow'd you more,
> And woman less of wit than heretofore?
> We once were famed in story, and could write
> Equal to men; cou'd govern, nay, could fight.
> We still have passive valour, and can show,
> Wou'd custom give us leave, the active too,
> Since we no provocation want from you.

In the epilogue to her play, *Sir Patient Fancy*, probably written in 1677, Aphra Behn confronted head-on the prejudices of her audiences and her fellow-playwrights. She knew only too well what she was talking about. The first Englishwoman to earn her living by writing, she was a trail blazer – and, given the state of the trail, there was a lot of blazing to be done.

Unlike her aristocratic predecessors, like Katherine Philips and Margaret Cavendish, Aphra Behn didn't shrink from exposing herself to the world's gaze. For one thing, she couldn't afford to: her livelihood depended on marketing her wares. For another, she had a lot to say about how the world conducted itself, both in public and in private, and she had no intention of keeping her insights to herself.

Although she drew misogynistic fire in her own time, this bold, brave woman was the target for even more outspoken attacks long after her death. One Victorian commentator described her work as 'a reproach to her womanhood and a disgrace even to the licentious age in which she lived'. But much worse than that has been the resounding silence, broken only by the occasional sneer, with which critics and commentators up to our own time have favoured her. The fact that her writing is strong, witty and intensely original somehow has never seemed to count for much. Her contemporaries at least had the sense to recognise that, like it or not, they were faced with a major talent; many indeed thought it not improbable that there might be a 'female laureate' in their time.

There are many mysteries and uncertainties surrounding Aphra Behn's life. One thing, however, is sure; and that is, that she can rarely have suffered from boredom. Penury, yes; unhappy love; fear of imprisonment; professional frustration; political treachery – but few of her days can have been dull. Growing up during the Civil War and the interregnum, she was in her early twenties when Charles II regained his kingdom in 1660. In mysterious circumstances, she then went to Surinam in South America. The ostensible reason for this journey has vanished; but the fruits of it are to be found in her exotically set story, *Oroonoko*, one of the earliest English novels. On her return to England, she seems to have married the Mr Behn who gave her her name; what else he gave her, if anything, is quite unknown since she makes little mention of him anywhere in her writings. In any case, Mr B. seems to have died or disappeared after only a year.

Following this, round about 1666, she put into practice her devout loyalty to the Stuart cause and agreed to go on a spying mission to Flanders, with the aim of gleaning information from the English rebels in Holland and, if possible, converting the most prominent anti-Royalists to Charles's cause. Floundering in the complex web of Anglo-Dutch politics, and unsustained by government help, she fell heavily into debt. Her powerful friends at court allowed this situation – one which distressed her greatly – to continue to the point where, on her return to England, she was forced into debtors' prison.

Shortly after her release, she came to her momentous decision to earn her own living by writing. Against a remarkable number of odds, she was extremely successful in this over a long period of time, acquiring fame as a dramatist, poet and novelist. Her close friends included the most prominent literary figures of the day.

In some ways, Aphra Behn's life has a peculiarly modern feel to it, despite the gulf of centuries. Here was a woman who wrote openly – and with wit – about sex; a woman who admired the achievements of other women; a woman who took pleasure in sexual ambiguity; a woman who saw no reason to disqualify herself from writing about affairs of state as well as affairs of the heart and other organs.

ALL THAT..
8. Nothing Changes
DOWN THERE
APHRA BEHN, COMMENTING IN 1682 ON WOMAN'S HEALTHY SEXUAL APPETITE, IMPLIED MEN MIGHT NOT BE ABLE TO..COPE
..the paleness of his face, the lankness of his cheeks, the thinness of his calves...
BUT RICHARD BURTON (ANOTHER ONE) EXPRESSED THE USUAL VIEW IN 1621...
'of woman's unnatural, insatiable lust, what country, what village, doth not complain?
THE IDEA OF THE BODY AS A PLUMBING SYSTEM, NEEDING THE ODD BIT OF REGULATION, -GAINED CURRENCY, & 'TOO LITTLE' SEX WAS FELT TO BE ALMOST AS BAD AS TOO MUCH...
look-if you don't like it, it must be doing you good!
..& VIRGINITY AS AN IDEAL HAD EASILY BEEN OVERTAKEN BY 'CHASTITY IN MARRIAGE' AS THE MOST DESIRABLE STATE - ESPECIALLY FOR WOMEN..
there's something wrong with this whole scenario...
PASSIVITY IN A WIFE WAS AN ASSET (TO WHOM?). WHEN THE RESPECTABLE MIDDLE CLASSES REALLY GOT GOING, IT WASN'T SO MUCH AN OPTIONAL EXTRA AS A STANDARD FITTING...
..& how the hell d'you think I'm getting up there in this lot?
the HANDY Pedestal Co! get yours now!

Jobs for Women
Believe me, Branwell, nobody's going to copy anything..
13 · Novelist
Jobs for Women
14 · Artist
Jobs for Women
Never mind love, I'll bet Virginia Woolf had bad days...
15 · Poet

Fig A.) Ye 'Fruit & Maggott' Coffee House, Fleet Street

MODULE 9

Enlightenment: bluestockings and best friends

Gather round, girls (Georgie, stop *doing* that) and let's consider all we know (and don't know) about the eighteenth century.

QUIZ

Do you:
(a) like the houses?
(b) hate the books?
(c) get in a hell of a muddle over the Hanoverian succession?
(d) agree with nearly everything that Mary Wollstonecraft says, if only you could remember what that was?

OK, well at least we're on common ground. Let's now take a settle in one of these famous coffee houses and listen to the talk of the day. You may have it vaguely in mind that the chaps drove hard bargains with each other over shares in heavily laden ships; engaged in vehement and well informed political discussion; hotly debated the vices and virtues of the latest novels to hit the booksellers; and suchlike. Maybe so. But it should be remembered that the same coffee-house society which avidly devoured the stimulating new *Spectator* also provided the main readership for the rather earlier *Tatler*. Could it not be, then, that coffee-house conversation was more likely to follow rather different channels? (Fig. A.)

There is no question, however, that valuable information *was* available in these places; and it seems a pity to think of it all being wasted. So perhaps we should take another look at some conversations possibly taking place elsewhere in the same building. (Fig. B.)

The gruesome fact remains, however, that as the century progressed, so to speak, so the opportunities for women's education and advancement seemed to diminish in scope and depth. Traditional women's trades – such as tailoring, shoe-making, blacksmithing, milling and butchering – were increasingly prohibited to women; while young middle-class women were steered towards 'accomplishments' rather than the training in accountancy, housekeeping and the classics which their mothers had sometimes been lucky enough to have experienced.

Fig. B.) Ye Kitchen of Ye 'Fruit & Maggott.

QUIZ

What do you understand by the term 'accomplishment'?
Would you include:

(a) the ability to perform a lethal neck-chop on a male attacker?
(b) a keen ear for the Aeolian harp?
(c) a neat hand at chain stitch?
(d) fairly dividing bills in restaurants?

How many of these attributes do you yourself possess? If none, perhaps you'd like to make your own list of personal accomplishments: there's no point in moping, after all. And a demoralised reader is no good to us. We still have to drag you – fighting and kicking if necessary – through some pretty sticky patches until we get you into the twentieth century.

Right, assuming that you got at least some of the right answers – and, no, they didn't include (a) – we'll proceed to look at a number of women who added 'learning' to their list of accomplishments. Some very well-heeled, others merely heeled, these women set up literary salons in order to provide themselves with an alternative to the mind-blowing inanities accompanying the card-games ubiquitous in their stratum of society. The bluestockings – for, yes, it was they – encountered rancour and scorn, bitter reproach and much contemptuous amusement. As Lady Mary Montagu, one of their number, had observed early in the century, 'There is hardly a creature in the world more despicable or more liable to universal ridicule than a learned woman.'

As ever, the more stupid and unlearned the men, the more vehemently they directed their indignation and scorn at the aberrant women. But even the male 'lions' of the salons, like Samuel Johnson and Horace Walpole, were often unable to resist cheap Boys' Own jibes at the expense of clever girls. It was fortunate then that the women took each other very seriously indeed. Elizabeth Montagu, known as the Queen of the Blues, commented in 1785 to her fellow hostess, Mrs Vesey, that their gatherings were attended by 'the best, the most accomplished, and most learned women of any times.'

Certainly, they do sound a very lively lot. Not only did Elizabeth Carter, distinguished Greek scholar, walk at least ten miles daily but she also took snuff and wrote eight to twelve hours a day, binding wet towels round her head and stomach and chewing green tea in order to keep awake. James Boswell, chronicler of Dr Johnson, a great friend of Miss Carter, further reports that, '... the learned Mrs Carter, at that period when she was eager in study, did not awake as early as she wished, and she therefore had a contrivance, that, at a certain hour, her chamber-light should burn a string to which a heavy weight was suspended, which fell with a strong sudden noise; this roused her from sleep and then she had no difficulty in getting up.'

Having been taught French, Latin, Greek and Hebrew by her father, Elizabeth Carter went on to improve the shining hour by teaching herself Spanish, German, Portuguese and Arabic. She also wrote poetry, her first published verse appearing in *The Gentleman's Magazine* when she was 17 years old.

Self-check question

If you had hit on the idea of chewing green tea, do you think that your intellectual life could have been very different?

'Mrs' Elizabeth Carter and an ear alarm clock

Miss Carter also found time (how? when?) to write copious and lively letters, pursue a number of intensely romantic friendships with other women, and avoid marriage altogether. (The 'Mrs' was a 'courtesy' title.)

Even when marriage was not avoided by members of the group, it seemed often to be ignored with some success. Lady Mary Wortley Montagu, for example, spent little time with her husband; but made good use of the comparative freedom granted to a married woman by travelling extensively and achieving a considerable reputation as essayist, poet and letter writer. Elizabeth Montagu (no relation) had been married at the age of 22 to a man of 51 and seems to have found in him little but 'churlishness' and an 'acid spirit'. The Queen of the Blues infinitely preferred to seek out the company of Elizabeth Carter, a close friend, and to preside over her dazzling parties. Her view of marriage was succinctly expressed in a letter to a friend: 'I am so much of Solomon's mind that the end of a feast is better than the beginning of a fray, that I weep more at a wedding than a funeral. . . .'

A spirit of rivalry was not unknown among the many bluestocking coteries, overlapping as they often were; and it may come as no surprise to learn that some of the initiated took pleasure in mutual antipathy. Dr Johnson's friend, Mrs Thrale, for example, only modified her intense dislike of Hannah More, writer and social reformer, when it became clear that Miss More was one of the few luminaries willing to countenance the widowed Mrs Thrale's re-marriage to an Italian musician.

Self-check question

Do you believe that only a pre-feminist consciousness could have allowed such petty interruptions to the tranquil flow of female harmony? Look in the mirror: could *you* find it in yourself to loathe a sister?

OK, OK, we take that question back. Please replace all the pages dislodged when you so precipitously hurled your book at the fireplace. And, no, we can offer no compensation for that charming family heirloom: collective responsibility in our view cannot be held to extend to an empty bottle of champagne commemorating the triumph of sensuality over reason.

As we were saying, the imp of malice had a good many friends amongst the bluestockings. And, indeed, the little beast seems to have scampered with joy over a good deal of the eighteenth century. Lady Louisa Stuart, for example – a luminary more social than intellectual – not only described the celebrated Lladies of Llangollen, whom she had never met, as of the 'genus mountebankum' but delivered herself of the following description of Elizabeth Montagu: 'She was a woman of great vivacity, no small store of wit, a competent portion of learning, considerable fame as a critic, a large fortune, a fine house and an excellent cook. Observe the climax,' said the Lady, 'it is not unintentional.'

What a relief then to turn to contemplation of the positive rage for romantic friendship which characterised so many of the bluestocking circles, and seemed to spread in interesting waves through much of the eighteenth century. 'Miss Talbot is absolutely my passion; I think of her all day, dream of her all night, and one way or other introduce her into every subject I talk of.' So wrote the young Elizabeth Carter in 1741, heralding the beginning of a close friendship that was to last until Catherine Talbot's death some 30 years later. An early letter from Miss Carter to Miss Talbot confirms the intensity of the feelings involved:

> People here are not in the least danger of losing their wits about you, but proceed as quietly and as regularly in their affairs as if there was no such person in being. Nobody has been observed to lose their way, run against a door, or sit silent and staring in a room full of company in thinking upon you, except my solitary self, who (as you may perceive in the description) have the advantage of looking half mad when I do not see you, and (as you know by many ocular proofs) extremely silly when I do.

QUIZ

What does the term 'romantic friendship' mean to you:

(a) the relationship between Shula and Caroline in 'The Archers'?
(b) never having to say you're sorry
(c) always having a screaming row on Saturday nights?
(d) a yearly exchange of Christmas cards?
(e) living together for 50 years and never spending a night apart?

Hmm ... well, perhaps you should all get together some time. Had you thought of a self-help group?

But you may be comforted to learn that our eighteenth-century romantic friends shared the odd row, tiff, sniff, tear, etc. Catherine Talbot, for instance, responded with something less than rapture when, on one of Elizabeth Carter's many jaunts abroad, Miss Carter wrote to her of the fascinating foreign women she was meeting. Taking her worries to a mutual friend – a bishop no less – Miss Talbot finds few grounds for comfort. She writes to her gadding friend that the bishop has pronounced that, 'You are only fallen in love with another woman and the first is forgot. A pretty gentleman you will come home indeed. Fi volage!'

ACTIVITY

Write a letter to a close friend which includes the telling use of the phrase, 'Fi volage!'.

Contemporary diaries and letters of middle- and upper-class women attest to the widespread – and heartfelt – importance given to close friendships in the eighteenth century. '... Your friendship is the only happiness of my life; and whenever I lose it, I have nothing to do but to take one of my garters and search for a convenient beam.' So wrote Mary Pierrepoint (later Lady Mary Wortley Montagu) to Anne Wortley in 1709. Can you be crass enough to reflect that the author couldn't have been driven to this extreme too often since in later years secure stockings of the blue hue were to figure prominently in her life?

Certainly, there could have been no question of feeling isolated or misunderstood. Every second literate woman seems to have been either scaling the heights of feeling or plumbing the depths. Take Elizabeth Montagu and Mrs Vesey, for example; Mary Wollstonecraft and Fanny Blood; Harriet Bowdler and Elizabeth Smith; Eleanor Butler and Sarah Ponsonby (the Ladies of Llangollen); and, perhaps in a class of her own, the ever susceptible Anna Seward. A distinguished poet, Anna Seward first lost her heart to a girlhood friend and continued to develop passionate attachments to other women for the rest of her life. The least one can say is that these women had *stamina*.

Needless to say, later commentators (heavens, yes, they *were* mostly men – how did you guess?) have gone to some lengths to explain away – or, if in a charitable mood, just explain – what was going on. The favourite explanations seem to include the following:

(a) It's all just a matter of language. An effusive style was the order of the day, so none of these women ever meant what they said.
(b) Somewhere in the background there was always a man (brother, husband, etc.) who was the *real* object of the passion.
(c) Men and women had completely different types of upbringing and so had little in common.
(d) Eighteenth-century women were a load of raging perverts, God knows why.

ACTIVITY

Strike out the explanations you don't like and substitute your own.

Now, before you run away with the idea that such friends did nothing but sigh, write emotional letters and gaze together at ruined abbeys in the moonlight, let the point be made that the ideal of romantic friendship contained hefty doses of self-improvement and charitable activity. A novel published in 1762, *A Description of Millenium Hall,* provided a popular focus of such ideals. Written by Sarah Scott, a woman unusual in being able to live out her ideal of romantic friendship, the novel describes how two women friends retire to the country and set up a self-sufficient 'model' community. They employ only servants who have handicaps and are therefore likely to find difficulty in obtaining other employment; they provide a home and useful training for impoverished gentlewomen; they offer a refuge to the aged and the orphaned; they set up a carpet factory and so, presumably, reduce the regional unemployment figures; and they make available most of the welfare and housing benefits which our Britain of the 1980s seems to have cast aside as outmoded and unnecessary. They also enjoy together 'rational' pleasures.

Self-check question

Do you have any pleasures that could remotely be described as 'rational'?

Younger sister of Elizabeth Montagu, Queen of the Blues, Sarah Scott had entered upon a marriage which, proving both disastrous and short-lived, nevertheless provided her with an income for life. This income allowed her 'retirement' (a fashionable concept) with her friend, Lady Barbara Montagu, to a house near Bath, where they ran a school for poor children. The school became the foundation of the Millenium Hall story.

Emergency self-check question

Have you, like all normal readers, totally lost track of which Montagu is which? If so, do you still think that you would have passed the bluestockings' Common Entrance exam?

The novel proved immensely successful, running into four editions by 1778. Few romantic friends, however, were in a financial position to follow the blueprint laid down, much as they might sigh and dream. Eleanor Butler and Sarah Ponsonby were among those who schemed, planned, manoeuvred, persisted, insisted and fought to achieve a secluded life together. It is not known whether these famous Ladies of Llangollen were familiar with *Millenium Hall*; but the life they established together shared much of the novel's philosophy. They lived according to a self-imposed 'system' which involved devoting themselves to self-improvement; avoiding the trivial pursuits of 'society' (of the high variety); beautifying their surroundings; staying firmly put in these same surroundings; and giving as much aid and succour as they could to the poor and unfortunate.

Self-check question

Do your relationships often involve a 'system'?

Oh.

Eleanor Butler was aged 29 when she first met Sarah Ponsonby, then a schoolgirl of 13. A mutual delight in books and dislike of society led the two upper-class Irishwomen into a close friendship. When, some years later, family pressures threatened to separate the friends, they resorted to a scandalous (and unsuccessful) elopement. Resolute amidst the subsequent cries of havoc, they eventually managed to persuade their respective families that they would be less trouble abroad than at home. In 1778, therefore, they left Ireland for ever and shortly afterwards settled in Llangollen Vale in Wales. They were to live there together until Eleanor Butler's death, 49 years later.

You want to know why they were so famous anyway? The reasons given seem to include the following:

(a) the belief (mistaken) that they went about dressed like men;
(b) admiration of lives of extraordinary faithfulness, harmony and constancy;
(c) the conviction (mistaken) that they never spent a single night away from home;

(d) fascination with the stream of distinguished guests who visited them in their later years together;
(e) incredulity that two women could make each other happy for more than 50 years;
(f) envy of lives which, though by no means devoid of financial worries, were dedicated to seclusion and self-sufficiency.

Lady Eleanor Butler wearing the Croix St. Louis. Why the award was made has never been totally clear . . .

ACTIVITY

Make an immoderate attack on the reasons that you find despicable, then jot down your own feelings about the life led by the Ladies.

Please now develop a catch in your voice and a slight haze of tears in your eyes (if you wear contact lenses, you may wish to remove them at this point). You are about to leave the Golden Age of Romantic Friendship. (Don't worry, though: there'll still be the odd thing to interest you in subsequent centuries.) Before you drift away, however, you may like to meditate on some of the common symptoms of romantic friendship. Can you put your hand on your heart (or anyone else's) and say that you are quite, quite immune?

Checklist

- A desire to 'retire' from this sordid world
- Vows to love eternally, and to live and die together
- An urge to grow roses and keep a cow
- A yen to elope
- An uncontrollable desire to read aloud to another person
- A tendency to migraines
- A highly strung and sensitive nature
- A belief that men can never really 'understand'

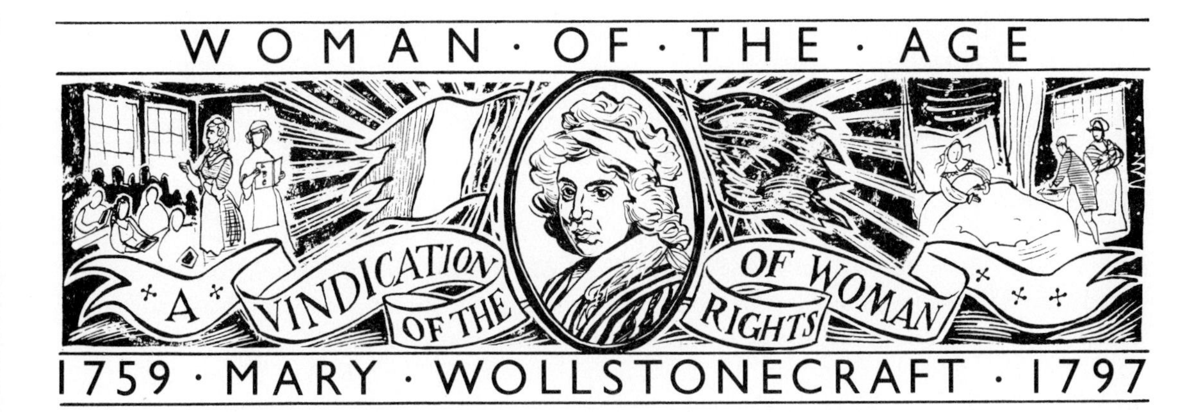

WOMAN · OF · THE · AGE
A VINDICATION OF THE RIGHTS OF WOMAN
1759 · MARY · WOLLSTONECRAFT · 1797

It's difficult to contemplate Mary Wollstonecraft's life with any equilibrium; indeed she never managed to do so herself. Prey to violent swings of mood, she was yet a firm believer in the power of reason and the will; acknowledged in the end to be one of the truly original thinkers of her time, she yet served a gruelling and classically female apprenticeship of companion, schoolmistress and governess; her own education neglected by everyone but herself, she wrote extensively on the need for women to gain education and employment opportunities equal to those open to men. And then, of course, there was her early death, at the age of 38 – a relentlessly old-style woman's death, from septicaemia following childbirth.

Born to a rather downwardly mobile family, Mary Wollstonecraft never really took to any of her blood relations, though she continued to give several of them support of one kind or another until her death. Her father was feckless, her mother passively miserable, light only breaking through when her eye fell on her adored eldest son who, predictably enough, grew up rich but horrid. 'A sense of grievance,' Mary Wollstonecraft's biographer, Claire Tomalin, suggests, 'may have been her most important endowment'.

Early passionate attachments to girlhood friends culminated in a dream of domestic bliss with Fanny Blood, a friend suffering from a family even more feckless than Mary's. Though Mary's soul was fired with romance, poor Fanny's was probably more intent on bare survival: not only was she desperate to get away from her father but she was also trying to come to terms with her engagement to a highly unreliable man.

Eventually, Mary's determination led to an establishment being set up – a school in Newington Green shared with Mary's sister, Eliza, and altogether too few pupils. Teaching, then as now, was not an easy way to make a living. The neighbours, however, were a revelation – real, live Dissenting intellectuals who advocated radical reform of society. For the first time, Mary had found company which encouraged her to think, talk and, later, write. But other circumstances were far from propitious. Fanny was suffering from consumption and was soon to die, shortly after her long-delayed marriage in Portugal. Mary made the journey to be at her child- and death-bed. And then the school failed, forcing Mary to take a position as a governess in Ireland. Before she did this, however, she secured a publisher's advance for her first book, *Thoughts on the Education of Daughters*.

Although at least one of her pupils liked her, the aristocratic parents certainly did not. They were not accustomed to governesses who, when they believed themselves insulted, sulked in their rooms and who generally seemed to think that they should be afforded just as much courtesy as anybody else.

Encouraged to return to London by her publisher, Joseph Johnson (another Dissenter), Mary did so, with the manuscript of *Mary*, her first novel, tucked in her handbag. The account of a rebellious young woman's kicking over at least some of society's traces, this work marked the beginning of Mary Wollstonecraft's career as a full-time writer. Mixing now with the radical likes of William Blake, Joseph Priestley and Thomas Paine, Mary undertook translations and reviews for Johnson's journal, *The Analytical Review*. When Edmund Burke produced his *Reflections on the French Revolution* in 1790, Mary shot back at him with her *Vindication of the Rights of Men*, a polemical work aimed at defending ideas of social progress and civil equality. And then in 1792 she published her *Vindication of the Rights of Woman* in which she took the radical step of applying similar arguments to the position of women. The enslavement of one sex by the other, she suggested forcefully, degraded all parties equally. And much, much more.

Naturally, it all provoked a storm of controversy. But the 'hyena in petticoats', as Horace Walpole described her, had better things to do than stick around and argue. Miserable as a result of an unsatisfactory love affair, she set out for revolutionary Paris. Remaining there for some time, Mary was shaken by the tumultuous course of the Terror, but remained confident that things would 'find their level'. She was shaken too by a new love affair – with Gilbert Imlay, an American, who gave her a child but also a monumental and long-lasting heartache.

On her return to England, she struggled to achieve some kind of reconciliation with him but got nowhere. Even her subsequent suicide attempt was unsuccessful. In between times, however, she went on a journey to Scandinavia with her young child and nurse and wrote a marvellous book about her visit. Oh yes, she *was* a remarkable woman.

Giving Imlay up as a lost cause, Mary looked about her again, renewed old friendships and began to re-establish her life. Her marriage in 1797 to the philosopher, William Godwin, was a rather embarrassing occasion for them both since each party was known to have strong reservations about the desirability of marriage as an institution. However, Mary was pregnant again and no doubt weary of scandal. At any rate, the ménage they established was a somewhat unconventional one, with each partner taking care to allow the other privacy and freedom; and her changed marital status did not prevent Mary from embarking on a new novel, *The Wrongs of Women*. She didn't live to complete it, however, dying after giving birth to her second child.

Her first daughter, Fanny, committed suicide when a young woman. Her second, Mary, grew up to write *Frankenstein* and to marry Percy Bysshe Shelley.

Vesta Victoria · Ruby Murray · Anne Shelton
The Ladybirds · Helen Terry · Annie Lennox · Alison Moyet
The Guest Stars · Miss Bluebell · Tracey Ullman · Jade
Variety
Hetty King 1883-1972 Male Impersonator
Hilda Baker Comedienne
Dame Gracie 1898-1979 Singer · Comic
Marie Lloyd 1870-1922 Queen of Music-Hall
Vesta Tilley 1864-1952 Male Impersonator
Florrie Forde 1876-1940
Nellie Wallace 1870-1948
Renée & Billie Houston · Comedy duo
Elsie & Doris Waters · Comedy - 'Gert & Daisy'
Helen Shapiro girl pop star (14)
Jessie Matthews Singer, Actress & Film Star
Victoria Wood Writer, Singer, Comic
Dame Vera Lynn b. 1917
Winifred Atwell · Pianist
Alma Cogan Singer...
Julie Goodyear
Doris Speed
Jean Alexander
Violet Carson
'CORONATION STREET'
Noele Gordon Soap & Variety
Shirley Bassey of Tiger Bay
Diana Dors Actress
The Beverley Sisters
Dusty Springfield Chanteuse
Hattie Jacques
Ivy Bensons All-Girl Band
Toyah Wilcox Actor · Singer

MODULE 10

More than One Nation: The Return of Victorian Val (excerpt)

Just what would we do without fiction to shed light on fact? (Doze on; you don't have to answer that.) For those whose eyes brighten at the thought of nineteenth-century industry and thrift but who have scrimped recently on their Dickens, Thackeray, Disraeli, and so on (aren't books a *price*?), here's a lovely surprise. At great personal expense, we've managed to get our hands on an extract from a little known Victorian 16-decker novel which, once again, explodes the phoenix-like myth that, amongst other industrial processes, the Victorians patented morality.

The Return of Victorian Val

Picture the scene if you will. (If you won't, don't.) Behold a thronged London street, with wave upon wave of humanity breaking upon its muddy shores. What flurry is there! What excitement! What variety of human experience! Fine ladies and gentlemen in fine costumes step from their carriages only yards from the spot where poor hawkers sell their pitiful wares. ('Forgot your lighter, sir? Try some of my byootiful matches – produced in the most economical conditions!'); while a little rag-clad girl, quite blue from the cold but with the pinkest nose imaginable, cries, 'Four bunches a penny, watercresses.' Poor child! Who will buy watercress in such bitter weather as this?

Huddled in the doorway of a bookshop we see the figure at the heart of our present tale. Her mouth working as she tries to make out the letters on a book in the window, she stamps her feet meanwhile to make sure that her blood moves as well. 'J-A-N-E E-Y-R-E', spells out Victorian Val – for it is she – 'written by C-U-R-R-E-R B-E-L-L'. Her eyes tired, she turns back to the street life around her, sighing as she does so, 'It's all right for them men in carriages; they can read and write when they're even littl' uns, no expense spared. And then when they're grown, why – there the world is, with a bright smile on its face, just waiting for their words.' She murmured something else as she bent to pick up her bundle and, if the gentle reader chooses to interpret the indistinct mutter as 'Bloody cheek', then he may not be too far mistaken.

Her feet, stoutly shod in heavy boots, seem weary; her path aimless; her eyes turn again and again to scour the set and impassive faces which pass her by in such quick and indifferent succession. Surely this must be a country girl come to town for the first time, wrapped still in the rough clothes of her native shire? (Yes, it is!) She is a working girl, certainly – that much is clear from her dress and manner; and she is not among the youngest of girls of this type: her strong limbs and well-developed form proclaim her to be at least sixteen years of age.

As dusk falls, she walks still, looking, it seems, for some kind of shelter – and perhaps for a friendly word or smile to warm the harsh stone which everywhere surrounds her. Though her belongings are few, the constant weight of her bundle forces even her strong shoulders to droop! Many gentlemen – some fine and some far from that state – attempt to greet her as she passes, but the two short words which she utters to each of them cause even these bold interlocutors to shrink away hastily. Her Dame School knew well perhaps the arts to teach young girls!

In her ignorance of these strange streets, Val finds her boots leading her into a fashionable square where, outside the grandest house of a very noble collection, a lady is being helped down from her carriage. The little dog which accompanies her is clearly affectionate but perhaps somewhat in-bred; why else would he be stupid enough to throw himself – as he does – under the abstracted Val's heavy tread? 'Oops, sorry, missus,' exclaims the country girl at once, wisely resisting the urge to kick the hairy spider-like creature even further from her person. After fluttering investigation has persuaded her that her darling's only injury is to his pride (and that serious enough, of course!), the lady turns a sharp eye on our heroine. 'And on what errand do you find yourself here, my girl?' she asks, sternly. 'I'm on no errand, missus, worse luck,' responds Val, with a sigh. 'I'm lost and that's a fact – though how I could be *found* in London, I don't know rightly know, since I've never been here before in my life and I don't know a living soul, far less a place to call *home*, even for a night.' 'I *see*,' said the lady – though

what it was that could have afforded her ocular proof of anything Val was at a loss to understand. However, when the lady – respectable, certainly, since her dress was of sober, if gilt-edged, hue – instructed the girl to follow her inside the mansion, Val was nothing loth: her feet were killing her.

The parlour into which she was led made as profound an impression on Val as would the living quarters of a Turkish Ottoman. The effects on her were not confined to the visual – though shine, richness and plenitude dazzled her momentarily; an even sharper impression was conveyed by the barking of her shins against an object that *looked* soft and yielding yet delivered a relentless blow. 'A table leg!' gasped Val, nursing her bruise.

Her artless words seemed to have delivered a blow of equal force to the lady's tender susceptibilities. 'A *table*, yes,' she murmured, as she fanned herself vigorously. 'Sit down, my girl,' she continued – a little faintly, it seemed to Val; but what, after all, was so rude about a table leg? – 'and tell me your story. How is it that you are wandering alone in this dangerous city?'

'My father, missus,' said Val, somewhat distracted by the sight of a parlourmaid bringing tea and wonderful things to eat, 'was a woolcomber. But a consumption took him when I was five years of age and my mother, at her wit's end to keep us all, with her wages so poor, married again. He was a hard man, a brutal man, and I swore that when my poor mother needed me no longer, I would tarry not a day more in his house.' At this point, Val displayed some strong-looking teeth. 'I worked in the gangs in the fields – hard work, missus, starting early and ending late, all weathers, and only 4d a day at the end of it. Well, two months ago my mother had her last child and her last breath – and I left there as I'd sworn to do. In London, I thought, I'd learn a trade, find a new life, a proper life.' On the words, 'proper life', Val gratefully accepted the foodstuffs offered to her, losing all sense of her surroundings for a few moments.

The lady – Lady Ffilanthrop, as she had explained herself to be – looked thoughtful, even though there was no one there to look at her, Val being otherwise occupied. 'It is a pitiful tale, my child,' she said, 'though, sadly, not an uncommon one. But God has bestowed His blessing on you in two important ways. He has saved you from falling into evil company – and He has sent you to me. Now, let me see what would be best.'

With these words, Lady Ffilanthrop starting sorting through a mass of papers neatly piled on the table before her. 'Ah yes,' she murmured, 'The National Truss Society for the Relief of the Ruptured Poor – very important, but not perhaps the most appropriate in your case.' Val wriggled in her chair. 'And perhaps the same holds true for the Royal Humane Society, whose worthy aim is "to restore persons in a state of suspended animation".' Val looked alarmed. 'But what about The Society for Returning Young Women to Their Friends in the Country?' Lady Ffilanthrop enquired briskly. Val looked even more alarmed. Lady F. became a little tetchy. 'My dear child,' she observed, 'When the Almighty bestows His blessings, He does not expect the plate to be sent back to the kitchen. Remember, my dear, that, being poor, you must make every effort to be deserving.' Val wondered momentarily if she did indeed have a rupture coming on but, remembering the agitation caused by mention of the table leg, she refrained from articulating her thoughts.

'Now here is the very thing,' exclaimed Lady F., 'The London Ladies' Committee for Promoting the Education and Employment of the Female Poor. On their books at the moment they seem to have – let me see – yes, nail-making – though you would have to get on a coach for that, it's in the Black Country. Mmm, fairly long hours, I see, 6 a.m. to 9 p.m. . . . but it *is* piece work. And then there's brickmaking, of course, but, no, I see that there are moral objections levied against *that* trade.'

As Lady Ffilanthrop pondered over her papers, the parlourmaid announced the arrival of a gentleman – and somebody else. Lady F. picked up the visiting card and exclaimed 'Ah! Mr Munby! What a surprise! Show him in, Ellen.' The appearance of Mr Munby interested Val much less than did that of the 'somebody else'. A young woman clad in hooded bonnet of padded cotton, blue striped shirt, waistcoat, apron of striped cotton, fustian trousers and clogs (brass-clasped), she looked even more out of place in Lady Ffilanthrop's parlour than did Val herself. 'Perhaps she is a Hottentot for saving,' mused our heroine, having heard a little of the splendid spiritual rescue missions in the colonies. But it appeared not, since Mr Munby (of unremarkable appearance) had already begun to explain his mission to Lady F.

'These Lancashire pit brow lasses,' he was saying, 'know their own minds! They enjoy their work! A healthy life in the open air, with considerable independence; a chance to develop the muscles through sorting coal and filling and moving railway wagons. Just look at these arms!' At this, he seized his companion by her shoulder and elbow and jacknifed the limb. Her face remained impassive. 'Why should their employment be put in jeopardy, my dear lady, by the interference of London gentlefolk who know nothing of the work or the conditions that surround it? Pray excuse my passion, Lady Ffilanthrop, but the cause of these girls is very close to my heart.'

'Yes, Mr Munby,' replied Lady Ffilanthrop, 'I can see that very well.' She paused momentarily, then continued, 'And I know of the fine documentary work which you have undertaken for many years on the conditions of these and other working girls. By the way, I'm also excessively interested in the prototype of Rational Dress now standing before me. However, you must know that the Select Committee has very good reasons for wishing to investigate further this matter of female employment in surface work at the mines. Deputations of pit girls to London, such as the one you are currently leading, cannot solve the issue at a stroke; there are, after all, moral concerns involved – to do with the proximity of male and female workers.'

Her words fell on suddenly deaf ears, since Mr Munby's eyes had lighted fully on Val. 'My dear young woman,' breathed Mr Munby, 'what honest, hard-working hands you have! Tell me – what is your occupation? Hours? Activities? Pray go into the activities in some detail – physical movements, and so on. And when you've finished, you may perhaps like to accompany me to a photographer's shop where I shall be only too pleased to procure a likeness of you.' Val – an astute girl – knew instinctively that the two words which she had employed to such good purpose on the street would serve her ill in this new situation. She was saved, however, from the necessity of replying at all, since Lady Ffilanthrop hastened to re-capture the scrupulous commentator's attention by proffering the incentive, 'Tell me, Mr Munby, something about the work of the nailer-girls of the

Black Country.' The flood of words, of gestures, soon thundered into full spate. While one spoke and gesticulated, the other made notes, consulted files and tut-tutted, both meanwhile becoming quite pink of countenance.

The two girls saw their opportunity and took it, stealing first of all towards the door of the parlour then, through the echoing and empty hall, towards the magnificent front

door. When it had slammed nobly behind them, they took to their boots and clogs and ran – as fast as they could in the circumstances – until fashionable London began to falter and fall into the vernacular: the fine squares becoming quite suddenly thickly inhabited canyons of streets. The sight of a gin shop stopped them in their tracks and, of one accord, they flung themselves in and requested a lifesaver.

Each relaxed for the first time in some hours. 'Thank God I'm shot of that funny old geezer,' said Annie (for such was the pit girl's name); 'If he'd asked me one more question or offered to take one more photograph, I'd have clobbered him, by Christ I would! The others think he's a laugh and he *has* helped us out a bit, but – well, I'd rather shovel coal than talk to him.' Perhaps the thought of her arduous occupation prompted a sudden thirst, for upon these words, Annie took a gargantuan swig from her tankard. Val had always hated to see anyone drink on their own and once again on this occasion displayed her team spirit; adding, for good measure, that she herself was considerably relieved to be out of a situation where she could feel an overpowering urge to reveal rather less – or rather more – than the truth about herself. 'My stepfather wasn't that bad,' she confided to Annie. 'I only said that about him being a brute because I knew that's what the lady wanted to hear. I got bored really – that's why I wanted to come to London; there had to be more to life than that gang and those men.'

The two young women toasted each other once, twice and perhaps even more. In reluctant agreement with Lady Ffilanthrop's views, they concurred that a life on the streets was a mug's game – although there could be considerable scope at the top of the profession. The famous 'Skittles', for example, did very nicely, thank you, in the way

of money and freedom; her quaint appellation being derived from the occasion when she had accosted a group of drunken and jeering guardsmen with the words, 'Shut your bloody row or I'll knock you over like a row of skittles.'

They roared at that, but agreed at the end of it that, since 'gentlemen is much greater blackguards than what blackguards is', the occupation was rendered impossibly distasteful and dangerous. 'I'd rather shovel coal,' said Annie again, but less distinctly this time. 'And so would I,' exclaimed Val heartily; at which they drank another toast to celebrate. 'And,' said Annie, 'if the men won't let us into *their* union, then p'rhaps we should start our bloody own.' It took more than a hiccup to stop Victorian Val drinking to *that*.

Self-check questions

1 Did you know that Charlotte Brontë (of Haworth, England; author of the novels, *Jane Eyre, Villette,* and so on) began her literary career under the masculine-sounding pseudonym, 'Currer Bell'?

Yes? Clearly, *you* went to school before the Cuts.

No? Isn't it *hell* to be young? Go back and re-read p. 79; we'd hate you to miss any of our jokes.

2 Have you ever tried running in clogs? In your opinion, might such activities in Victorian times have given rise to the phrase, 'well-turned ankle'?

3 Can you explain in one paragraph how and why the above extract is grossly unfair to the female philanthropists of the nineteenth century?

Yes? Here's an apple for you; don't choke on it.

No? Go on then, write a book about it instead.

Mary Agnes Clerke
Jane Harrison
Dame Helen Gwynne Vaughn · Helen Marion Macpherson Mackay · Agnes Arber
Dorothy Garrold · Dame Kathleen Kenyon · Sarah Mapp
Science & Travel
Rosalind Franklin 1920 - 1958 helped discover DNA's structure
Ada Lovelace 1815 - 1852 'The World's First Programmer'
Jocelyn Bell b. 1943 Discovered pulsars
Caroline Herschel 1750 - 1848 Astronomer
Isabel Thorne Medical Student, 1869
Florence Nightingale 1820 - 1910 nursing, public health
Margaret Cavendish 1623-1673 populariser of science
Elizabeth Garrett Anderson 1836-1917 Est. London School of Medicine
Mary Kingsley 1862-1900 Singular Traveller
Joan Robinson. b. 1903 Professor of Economics
Mary Sidney 1561 - 1621 Chymist.
Isabella Bird 1831 - 1904 Fearless traveller
Dr. Miriam Rothschild b. 1908 Naturalist & flea expert
Dorothy Hodgkin b. 1910 Crystallography. Nobel Prizewinner
Sophia Jex-Blake 1840-1912 Doctor.
Mary Bruce 1849 - 1931 Microscopy
Mary Somerville 1780 - 1872 Mathematician
Mary Seacole 1805 - 1881 Healer & Traveller
Marianne North 1830 - 1890 Traveller & Artist
Lady Hester Stanhope. 1776 - 1839. Traveller, Arabist
Mary Anning 1800 - 1847 Geologist
Dame Freya Stark Traveller, Writer, Arabist. b. 1893
Daphne Jackson. b. 1936 1st woman professor of physics (& only)
Jacquetta Hawkes b. 1910 Archaeologist

MODULE 11

Out of the Parlours and into the Prairies: Victorian women travellers

People can only stand so much peace and quiet. Even women can only stand so much peace and quiet. Think about it for a moment.

QUIZ

You're sitting in the parlour listening to your mother tell you about the people who've just moved in five houses down the street. They're in cotton, it appears. You're in bombazine and something of a muck sweat, what with the fire burning merrily in the grate and bits of whalebone crushing your ribs. Your sampler seems to be getting damper and grubbier by the minute. Your sister is sulking and sighing in the corner because her friend, Elizabeth, has been taken shopping twice that day and she's only gone once.

Now indicate by ticks and crosses which of the following options you consider would be most likely to end your sense of suffocation:

- entry into an institution of higher learning
- purchase of a summer dress
- domestic murder
- a trip to Japan/Africa/the Rocky Mountains.

Your years of experience in answering magazine quizzes are at last coming in useful. You're right, of course – don't the Rocky Mountains sound terrific?

Isabella Bird thought so too when in 1873 she left off 'rioting most luxuriantly' in the 'congenial life of the wilds' in the Sandwich Isles (now Hawaii) and moved on to the chillier wilds of Colorado. Both were a far cry from the rectory parlours of her youth (she was 40 when she began her travels); both also seemed infinitely preferable (though she was actually very fond of her sister).

It wasn't that Isabella Bird despised the comforts of home. But her taste was not standard issue for middle-class women of her period. Consider her description of two of her resting places in the Rocky Mountains:

'It is quite comfortable – in the fashion that I like. I have a log cabin, raised on six posts, all to myself, with a skunk's lair underneath it, and a small lake close to it.'

And then, 'My room is easily "done", but the parlour is a never-ending business. I have swept shovelfuls of mud out of it three times today. There is nothing to dust it with but a buffalo's tail. . . .'

Self-check question

What was Isabella Bird's idea of 'home, sweet home'? Was she likely to have hung a sampler on the wall?

If you're not sure of the answers, go back and re-read the quotations. (Or have a drink – you're obviously in a bad state. In fact, come to think of it, feel free to pour one out for us too.)

Much admired in her own day – she was the first woman to be invited to speak to the Royal Geographical Society – Isabella Bird has come in for a considerable amount of neo-feminist fêting. Consider for a moment the description to be found in the jacket blurb to a recent edition of one of her books: 'A daring horsewoman, she rode a thousand miles in Morocco at the age of 69. She is buried in Edinburgh.'

Perhaps you'll agree that there is a splendid ring to this information? The daring and extraordinary exploits of the Victorian lady traveller are most satisfyingly framed by the moral rectitude of dying in a city noted for its lack of wildness.

It would be a trifle misleading to say that many other women followed in Isabella Bird's footsteps. For a start, you know how it is with history, some of the lady travellers came before her, others after. (No point thinking 'how messy'; that's how it was.) For another thing, it would have been damned difficult to follow in some of her footsteps – she specialised in truly out-of-the-way little spots. Read her *Unbeaten Tracks in Japan* and see for yourself why they remained unbeaten for so long.

The point is, however, (yes, we're getting there) that Isabella Bird was only one of a considerable number of women travellers during the nineteenth century. Many were British or American and came from jolly respectable homes.

Some, like the English Annie Taylor, hadn't much money but a lot of Good News to spread; she made determined and persistent assaults on the somewhat reluctant Tibetans. Others, like the American May French Sheldon and the English Marianne North, took more of an interest in exotic flora and fauna. May French Sheldon, whose serious exploration apparently took place 'when she circumnavigated Laka Chala in a copper pontoon', had a passion for big game hunting. She also was in the habit of carrying a pennant inscribed '*Noli me tangere*' (do not touch me) – a warning and admonition which must have puzzled all those natives who had not yet had the benefit of a missionary education with Latin. Marianne North took a rather gentler approach to her surroundings, spending much of her time painting plants and flowers. She was acutely upset

Marianne North, with Critics

and embarrassed on one occasion when it transpired that her meticulously accurate representation of a detached flowering bough showed the wretched thing growing upside down.

Not all the Victorian lady travellers were rich, well-born eccentrics; and few were merely that. Mary Seacole was something else again. Born in Jamaica in 1805 from a Scottish military father and a mother who, black and free, ran a boarding-house, Mary Seacole combined a commitment to medicine with a love of travel. Refused official permission to nurse in the Crimean War, she went on her own account, set up a provisions business and became a 'Crimean heroine' for the skill and courage displayed in her care for wounded and dying men.

Mrs. Seacole declining brisket of Iguana.... preferring spit-roast Parrot

Self-check question

Can you remember any of the names mentioned in the previous two paragraphs? Why?

Jot down the names of any other Victorian lady travellers you can think of.

Have you included Lady Hester Stanhope, Mary Kingsley, Lady Lucie Duff Gordon, Emily Eden, Fanny Bullock Workman?

Well done! (Write your own bloody book then).

ACTIVITY

Assemble the equipment you think a Victorian lady traveller might take with her. Here is a drawing of some of May French Sheldon's equipage to help you.

Could you fit this into your backpack?

Euphemia Maud TATTING
Suffering from langour & ennui left England in 1870. ~ Cured 15 minutes out of Dover, after casting her stays to the waters.
Intended for missionary service, was appalled by 'knock-on' effect of exported Christianity...
FEEDING INSTRUCTIONS
Finding herself in foreign parts, began global study of carniverous plants; sent many specimens to Kew.
Increasingly adopted native dress. Carried huge wardrobe of appropriate ethnic outfits
Became Photographer in India; had travelling darkroom fitted in howdah (She felt leeches would be less likely to ruin glass plates at this level.)
1877 ~ Was herself photographed by Julia Margaret Cameron, World's End, Ceylon
I think one day I shall write a book of 'Eccentrics'. Mrs Grote shall be one. Lady Hester Stanhope. Margaret Fuller. Duchess of Newcastle. Euphemia Maud Tatting. Aunt Julia?
Virginia Woolf's diary, 1915. 'Aunt Julia' (Cameron) presumably related her memories of Euphemia to the diarist's mother.
Known to Guatemalan Indians as 'She~Who~Wears~An~Armadillo~on~her~Head'
Met Mary Kingsley & took up anthropology, discovering several new humanoids including 'Self Sufficient Woman' & 'Incapable Man'
Fortnum &
After derision greeted her new classifications, EM Tatting returned to England to throw herself into the militant Suffrage campaign, often in Arab dress
Made her last trip to Africa (1917) ~ into German~occupied territory on a daring bat~ringing expedition
AFRICAN QU
Retired, after cessation of hostilities, near Basingstoke, to complete her great 13 volume work, 'With Bat, Bone & Tusk in 5 Continents'

You may like to meditate on the ingredients which went to make up a successful Victorian lady traveller – or 'globe trotteress', to borrow a phrase used by an eminent geographer of the time.

A sound constitution, you may suggest, for one. Surprisingly, perhaps, this seemed to prove less of an incentive (or excuse) for travelling than did ill-health. Ill-health, and the hope of alleviation thereof, propelled a good many future travellers out of the parlours and into the prairies.

Checklist

The following attributes seem to have helped:

- a tendency to ill-health
- devotion to Papa
- a reluctance to be told what to do
- the single state or an unconventional marriage
- rampant individualism

Can you find any examples of these in the preceding account of the life of Euphemia Maud Tatting, a little-known lady traveller (British)?

WOMAN · OF · THE · AGE
1833 · CHRISTIAN · WATT · 1923

Born into an ancient sea-faring family in Broadsea, a fishing village near Fraserburgh in north-east Scotland, Christian Watt lived a life of unbelievably hard work, courage, poverty, wit, great suffering, compassion, intellectual curiosity, strong religious faith, and social and political iconoclasm.

We know this because during her old age, spent quite sanely in Aberdeen's Cornhill Asylum for the Insane, she wrote extensive memoirs of her own life and that of her community. At that time she was offered the opportunity to 'go into the place for private patients as a reward for my life of hard work. There I would have a personal maid. That is like an old horse being put out to grass! I have no wish to be waited on, I will die in the yoke: this morning I peeled a bucket of tatties at 90. I am neither daft or dottled.'

Christian Watt came from a long line of strong and able women. 'My granny Gunner had plenty of money,' she comments, explaining that 'she possessed the chief ingredient for accumulating it, the greed of Auld Nick.' Christian's own, considerable, determination was channelled in rather different directions. For one thing, she wanted no advice on who might make a suitable husband for her. 'When I grew older my mother wanted me to marry Dunkie's Jock, who was a dull person I did not fancy pushing through life. If there was to be any choosing I was going to be the one who would do it.' For another, she resolutely rejected the life of domestic service yawning before her. She writes of an employer, Lady Saltoun: 'I went as her maid in the fall of 1843. She was pleased with my work and wanted me to come south with her, but I had no intention of accepting this life at everybody's beck and call. She offered me a dress length as a gift; I said I would rather have a dictionary. She thought it a strange request, but gave me one from the library. It opened up new realms in my life, for my nose was never out of it.'

In 1843, note, Christian Watt was 11 years old. She had gone into service at 8½ years of age. By the time she was 10 she had also learned another trade – how to gut fish quickly and expertly. She subsequently became laundry-maid in a local laird's house and in later years spent time in service both in London (where the poverty of the dockland shocked her) and New York (which she adored, though saw there the seeds of racial violence).

Christian Watt did not believe in accepting, meekly or otherwise, the assumptions so often underlying the mistress/servant relationship. 'I had tolerated [the housekeeper]

Macdowall for years addressing me as 'Watt', my surname. When I was older the worm turned, I replied to her question, "Yes, Macdowall" ... They might as well call you Fido or Whiskers. I think it the height of impudence and degradation to treat a human being as a dog or a cat.'

When working in one of the fine local houses, Christian became friendly with the son of the house, the Master of Lovat, known as Shemmy. Lord and Lady Lovat summoned Christian to the house to express their concern over such an unsuitable connection. Christian gives a breathtaking account of this interview, which included the following exchange between Lord Lovat and herself. 'He said, "This is a democracy, with reasonable opportunity for all", I said, "That is the biggest load of dirt since the dung cart went round the Broch gathering the dry closets yesterday".' But perhaps it was just as well that the quite innocent friendship did not lead to marriage: Shemmy, one can't help feeling, was not good enough for Christian Watt. One evening she asked him, 'Is not the creation of the world really so wonderful? Just fancy the mountains and all the billions of tons of water in the ocean hanging in space'. 'Shemmy,' she goes on to comment, 'was not interested in science.'

Those 'billions of tons of water' in fact dominated Christian Watt's life. She gutted fish, journeyed to the north to cook for the fishing fleet, travelled all round Buchan selling fish. She married a fisherman and worked with him on mending the nets and on the rest of the un-ending toil involved in wresting a living from an environment where danger and unpredictability lay not only in the weather but in economic trends. She lost four of her seven brothers at sea; and, in the course of time, she lost a 13-year-old son. Her husband too was drowned – in 1877 – leaving her with eight children, only one of whom was of an age to work (and he had already gone to sea).

It was at this point that Christian Watt first went 'for a rest' to Aberdeen Royal Mental Asylum. Contrary to common modern assumptions about nineteenth-century institutions of this kind, Cornhill was not a terrible place – though it housed terrible tragedy enough. The Physician Superintendent, says Christian, 'was a kindly, skeely man, genuinely interested in his patients.' And Cornhill itself 'was a blessed haven of peace as it has been a heaven to so many, and the lassies who look after the patients could not be kinder.' Characteristically, Christian goes on to add that, 'It is scandalous those quinies are paid with sweeties for doing such a noble job.'

Although Christian did return home from that first stay in Cornhill, she was back again before too long, her health, mental and physical, almost broken by the shock of her bereavements, the social ostracism consequent on her first stay in hospital, and the terrible battle to earn enough money to feed and clothe her children. During the next period at home, her 'reasoning broke', she says. 'I struggled to hang onto it, it was distinct as a butter plate breaking on the floor.' She was certified as insane and spent the rest of her life – some 45 years – at Cornhill.

The acute phase of her illness passed away relatively quickly. She comments that, 'The world is so unwilling to accept the disturbed mind functions in exactly the same way as the normal one. It is a tremendous problem the mind is trying to cope with; perhaps if I had been less of a thinker and a more dull person it might not have affected me in the same way.'

Although always concerned and often worried about her children (who were taken in by different friends and relatives), she went on to build up a rich life in the asylum, comforting and helping many and working hard as laundrywoman and as fishwife, going out to buy fish at Aberdeen Market. Over the years her visitors were legion – family, friends and several ex-employers. Her tart social and political comment continued unabated.

Dame Clara Butt · Music, Dance, Theatre · Sarah Walker
Valerie Masterson · Josephine Barstow · Elizabeth Welch · Ann Jellicoe
Rita Hunter Soprano b. 1933
Cleo Laine Jazz Singer b. 1927
Kathleen Ferrier 1912 – 1953 Contralto
Dame Ethel Smythe 1858-1944 composer
Elizabeth Lutyens 1906 – 1983 Composer
Jacqueline du Pré Cellist & Teacher b. 1945
Dame Janet Baker · Contralto b. 1933
STEINWAY
Sidonie & Marie Goossens Harpists
Thea Musgrave b. 1928 Composer
Dame Myra Hess Pianist 1890-1965
Joan Armatrading Singer-Songwriter b. 1947
Barbara Thompson Jazz Saxophone
Gwyneth Jones Soprano b. 1936
Jane Glover Conductor b. 1949
Dame Isobel Baillie b. 1895 Soprano
Dame Marie Rambert 1888-1981 Founder, Ballet Rambert
Lynn Seymour · Dancer
Dame Ninette de Valois b. 1898
Dame Margot Fonteyn · Ballerina b. 1919
Dame Alicia Markova (Alice Marks) · Ballerina
Moira Armstrong TV Director
Pam Gems Playwright
Lillian Baylis Founder, Old Vic 1874 1937
Verity Lambert · Producer
Michelene Wandor Playwright
Aphra Behn 1640-1689 Playwright
Joan Littlewood Director b. 1914 Theatre Workshop
Caryl Churchill · Nell Dunn · Shelagh Delaney

MODULE 12

'Snakes and Ladders' or *The Further Education Game*

Now, don't pretend that you've never played 'Snakes and Ladders' before – even if nowadays you may not like to think too much about the former. The Ladders (oh yes, *now* you remember) are the ones you climb up (hurrah!); the Snakes are the ones you slither down (boo!). All you need to start is a dice and a counter or token for each player (two might be cosy, but don't feel constrained – who are we to tell you how to live?)

You may like to give some thought as to what kind of counters would be most appropriate for this particular version of the game. Old prefect badges? Those mysterious bits that fell off your Swiss Army knife? Your badge saying, 'Grow your own dope; plant a man'?

SNAKES AND LADDERS
YOU TAKE A BRILLIANT FIRST! MOVE ON TWO SPACES 75
CHAPERONE IS LATE! CONFINED TO STUDY FOR ONE THROW! 76
A MALE VISITOR. YOU FAIL TO REMAIN STANDING & KEEP STUDY DOOR OPEN! 72
But he was talking for 3 hours, ma'am...
EARLY FOR LECTURES. G BEST SEATS ANNOY MA STUDENTS. THROW AGAIN.
MEET ELIZA-BETH GARRETT ANDERSON. DECIDE TO BE A DOCTOR! THROW AGAIN. 52
INHERIT FORTUNE. ENDOW WOMEN'S COLLEGE! 47
YOUR CHAPERONE PUTS HER PRICES UP. MISS A TURN WHILE THEY COME DOWN 46
DON FEELS THREATENED MARKS ESS DOWN. MISS TUR
Nasty, forward minxes!
GO TO NIGHT SCHOOL & BETTER YOURSELF! THROW AGAIN 25
DOCTOR SAYS STUDY WILL DAMAGE REPRODUCTIVE ORGANS... 28
They don't feel any different to me...
ROW WITH FIANCEE. MOVE ON 3.
a woman spoiled by education won't be a good mother of my sons! 23
ROW WITH FATHER. BACK 3 SPACES
Does tha not want to get a husband?
DROP OFF THROUGH BOREDOM IN LAUNDRY LESSON. 4
HIGH SCHOO SCHOLARSHI DISCOVER U HEALTHY INTEREST I UNIFORMS. MOVE ON 6 PLACES

THE FURTHER EDUCATION GAME
READING EUCLID UNDER THE BEDCLOTHES, YOUR CANDLE BURNS COLLEGE DOWN 79
80
MEDICAL FINALS. MALE STUDENTS PUT SHEEP IN EXAMINATION ROOM 81
82
83
YOU ARE ELECTED MISTRESS OF GIRTON!
CONGRATULATIONS!
66
O.D. ON COCOA. MISS TURN & RECOVER 65
64
63
CLASSICAL EDUCATION IS FRAGMENTED. DONS CUT OUT RUDE BITS. MISS TURN. 62
61
NOT ALLOWED INTO ANATOMY CLASS. BACK FOUR SPACES 55
56
HIGHER EDUCATION SAID TO PRODUCE FLAT CHESTS! 57
Sounds OK!
58
59
60
42
41
40
UNIVERSITY! MIDNIGHT FEAST IN HALL. HANGOVER. 39
38
37
ACCEPTED BY WOMEN'S UNIVERSITY COLLEGE! MOVE ON FIVE PLACES 31
32
33
34
MARRIED ♀'s PROPERTY ACT, 1882. YOU HAVE INDEPENDENT MEANS BUY YOURSELF OUT! 35
36
YOU DECIDE ON AN INDEPENDENT LIFE! BOLDLY GO FORWARD FOUR PLACES! 18
17
16
YOU HAVE A FAINTING FIT. RECOVER & THROW YOUR CORSET AWAY. THROW AGAIN. 15
14
13
7
READ 'SCHOOL' STORIES, & HAVE A RUSH OF TEAM SPIRIT TO THE HEAD. MISS TURN. 8
WIN UNIVERSITY SCHOLARSHIP! 9
10
FAIL TOTALLY IN 'WOMANLY ACCOMPLISHMENTS'! MOVE ON FIVE PLACES. 11
12

Jobs for Women
NATIONAL·UNION OF THREAD NEEDLE & BODKIN OPERATIVES
22 · Needleworker
Jobs for Women
It's not his running off I mind- it's his taking the horse..
23 · Bargee
Jobs for Women
24 · Knocker-Up

ALL THAT..
13
Back to the Womb
DOWN THERE
'WOMAN AS WILD ANIMAL' – IT WAS ALL BLAMED ON THE WOMB. THE MEDIEVAL IDEA OF THE WOMB MOVING AROUND THE BODY (THUS ACCOUNTING FOR WOMAN'S UNPREDICTABLE NATURE) - ONLY LOST GROUND IN THE 17TH CENTURY, WHEN DISSECTION WAS LESS PROHIBITED. (WHEN THE WOMB STOPPED OFF BY THE HEAD, THIS MEANT THINGS WERE REALLY HOTTING UP...)
how many times have I told you?! - Dont keep them in the bed?!!
look out... wombs on the move again...
SO, TO LURE THE WOMB BACK TO THE NETHER REGIONS, ODOROUS APPLICATIONS WERE ADMINISTERED
A Foul SMELL applied to NOSE
B Nice SMELL applied to nether parts
C Womb
IN MORE ENLIGHTENED TIMES, (DESPITE THE IDEA THAT ALL THAT WAS 'GREAT, NOBLE & BEAUTIFUL' WAS SAID TO RESIDE IN THE OVARIES) - A MUCH MORE SATISFYING CURE FOR HYSTERIA WAS TO REMOVE THEM ENTIRELY..
O.. wait till she's given you a son... then we'll have them out!
ANOTHER FANCIED REMEDY FOR HYSTERIA, INSANITY & AMENORRHOEA .. WAS CLITORIDECTOMY..
& how would you like castration to take care of your temper tantrums?
HIGHER EDUCATION WAS THOUGHT TO ATROPHY THE OVARIES (IF THEY HADN'T ALREADY BEEN WHIPPED OUT TO CURE SOMETHING ELSE..) & WOMEN WERE CONSIDERED ON PHYSICAL GROUNDS TO BE INCAPABLE OF VOTING
Well.. could'nt make their minds up 'oo to choose..
Uer... stands to reason..
IT WAS 'AS IF THE ALMIGHTY, IN CREATING THE FEMALE SEX, HAD TAKEN A UTERUS & BUILT UP A WOMAN AROUND IT...'
what happened to Adam's Rib all of a sudden?

MODULE 13

Suffragettes and All That

You all know about the suffragettes, of course, because, along with Boadicea, Queen Victoria and Florence Nightingale, they *are* the women of History, as he is generally understood. (Queen Elizabeth, it's been hinted, can't appear in the list because, frankly, she wasn't a Real Woman. Funny that.)

ACTIVITY

If any of you have sussed out the connection between hacking Romans to bits, not believing in fairies (sorry, lesbians), carrying a torch for wounded soldiers, and slicing policemen's braces, then please contact us, day or night; your information could be very valuable.

It's possible, however, that you may have underestimated the courage, dedication and sheer physical prowess displayed by the suffragettes. Consider, for example, the following account by Annie Kenney, cotton mill worker and suffragette leader, of meeting working women in London's East End:

> I don't know how I had the audacity to talk votes for women to those thin, sallow, pinched, poverty-lined faces. I enjoyed their quick tongues, their prying little gossips and their love of company. . . . To give no offence I would drink a cup of tea with every woman I called to see.

Self-check question

How many cups of tea could you drink even in the worthiest of causes? In your opinion, have feminist bladders become weaker over the years?

It may have appeared to you – as it has done to thousands of others – that the suffragettes sprang suddenly from the head of History, fully armed with umbrellas and boxes of matches. Of course, it wasn't like that. The militant Women's Social and Political Union was formed against the background of a long, respectable – and ultimately ineffectual – struggle to extend the franchise to women. Ever since 1865, when the first women's suffrage society was established in Manchester, women and sympathetic men had lobbied Parliament to give women the vote. By the early 1900s, many of the pioneer suffragists were dead or dead tired and the suffrage societies had lost their head of steam. The new militants who formed the WSPU were criticised strongly for their aggressive tactics – but many old-time suffragists also acknowledged that the movement had been re-vitalised.

Certainly, as the militant years went on, increasing numbers of women were swayed by the arguments for women's suffrage and, whether or not they approved of the suffragettes' approach to the issue, joined one or other of the societies set up to gain the vote for women. At the first great women's suffrage demonstration in 1906, members of trade organisations and suffrage groups from all over the country converged on London; and the deputation to the Prime Minister included the 76-year-old pioneer suffragist, Emily Davies, who had handed the first women's suffrage petition to John Stuart Mill in 1866. (By the way, she did *not* crown this career by throwing herself under the King's horse at the Derby – that was (the much younger) Emily Wilding Davison.)

W.S.P.U
VOTES for WOMEN!
..& this is our Miss ffinch, working her way through the Cabinet with a horsewhip! - Nearly had Mr Churchill this morning!

ACTIVITY

Jot down some reasons why 'suffrage' and 'the franchise' sound so much more desirable than 'the vote'.

Now, can you conceive of a movement which started off in great style, personified by powerful leaders; which thrilled and shocked press, politicians and public alike; which contained within its early solidarity germs of future divisions; which bitterly opposed the 'double standard' raised by men to the status of a law of nature; which insisted that oppression on grounds of sex cut across class lines? No, no – we're still talking about the early 1900s; though you may have a point.

The fight for the vote wasn't exactly a single-issue campaign; but it came pretty close to it. A devastating single-mindedness amongst the suffragettes enabled them to press their claims to other people's screaming point. Dorothy Pethick, a younger sister of Mrs Pethick Lawrence, WSPU luminary, describes her arrival in prison after a stone-throwing episode:

> We refused to change our clothes. They asked us what was our name – 'Votes for women'; our age – 'Votes for women'; what was our religion – 'Votes for women'. Our idea was to break the resistance of the prison staff, so they would say they couldn't do with us.

Few people, one imagines, either inside or outside prison, could 'do with' a truly determined suffragette.

Dr Ethel Smythe conducts Suffragettes singing the 'March of the Women' with a toothbrush in Holloway Prison . . .

March, march, swing we along . . . Strong & defiant . . .

VOTES for WOMEN

On another occasion, some youthful members of the WSPU decided to send 'a human letter' to publicise a forthcoming onslaught on the House of Commons. A clerk at the West Strand Post Office gave them the appropriate form (surely the most exciting event so far in her/his professional life) and the sender completed it carefully (perhaps the pens worked in those days), addressing her two colleagues to 'The Right Hon. H. H. Asquith, 10 Downing St., SW.'

The threepenny charge was paid, a telegraph boy was called, and the Letter set out on its way, the two women walking on either side of the boy and holding placards indicating their destination and message, 'Votes for women – Deputation – House of Commons – Wednesday.'

On being stopped by the police in Downing Street, the telegraph boy showed his way-bill and was ushered to the door, the Letter meanwhile being held back. Number 10's butler showed the boy in, but shortly afterwards His Master's Voice left his post in order to deal personally with the waiting Communication. 'You must be returned,' pronounced the butler; to which the Letter replied, 'But we have been paid for.' 'Well then,' returned HMV, 'the post office must deliver you somewhere else. You can't be delivered here.' The Letter knews its rights: 'But the express letter is an official document and must be signed according to the regulations.' The butler wasn't daft either: 'It can't be signed, you must be returned, you are dead letters.'

Self-check question

How do you think the butler might have reacted to the sight of a gorillagram?

It wasn't all fun and games, of course. While injustice and political chicanery galled the suffragettes' souls, revolting prison conditions and brutal force feeding tormented their bodies. But some of them found ingenious ways of preserving their equilibrium in jail:

> I have seen the doctor. He argued with me about the unreasonableness of our conduct. . . . The chaplain came. He was rather nice. He asked if there was anything I wanted. I said I wanted a good many things, and I supposed we would not be allowed a library book. . . . He said he was very sorry to see us here, and I couldn't keep back a few tears when he had gone. I feel so weak. A wardress brought in a Bible, Prayer Book and Hymn Book. I read the marriage service over. I thought it would get my blood up, so I read Paul's opinions on the duties of a wife.

The picture of yer average suffragette as a madcap middle-class girl has proved remarkably durable. But it was by no means necessarily so. Despite a concentration after 1907 on securing the support of upper-class women, the WSPU continued to attract members from all classes of society. The resolution, cool-headedness and courage displayed by women whose lives were already hard-pressed gives cause for considerable thought. Listen, for example, to the words of one WSPU member, Mrs Higginson from Lancashire, as she describes her domestic arrangements before departing for the WSPU's final national militant event, a deputation to the King in 1914:

> They told us months beforehand so we had time to make our preparations. We left our houses in very good condition and good baking behind us, and people who wouldn't go to prison would look after my children while I was away. One

> took a girl and one took a boy, and one came to look after my husband, and he arranged to have his holidays at that time.

Mrs Pankhurst and her redoubtable daughter, Christabel, ran a tight ship at the WSPU; and many feminists agreed neither with their objectives nor their tactics. Sylvia Pankhurst, the second daughter, felt herself forced into a painful split with her family as her commitment to the cause of working-class women clashed with the increasing reluctance of the WSPU to develop a radical focus on women's struggle (an uneasy neutrality which ended with Mrs Pankhurst's conversion to the Conservative cause). Other feminists, such as Dora Marsden, editor of the remarkable journal, *The Freewoman*, believed that the vote was something of a chimera, a token elevated to the status of a Holy Grail – and one which, like the Grail itself, would lead only to death and disappointment. Why fight for a stake in the system, such women argued, if the system itself is rotten to the core? Aren't there better ways of using your energy? (Like destroying the state, freeing the shackled human spirit, etc.)

ACTIVITY

Have a quiet drink with a few friends and argue like hell about who was right and who was wrong, why you wouldn't have made the same mistakes, and why so many women seemed to be in love with Christabel.

For better or for worse, people remember the suffragettes, and much contemporary feminist activity – to the joy of some and the fury of others – has been compared, contrasted and generally kicked about in the light of that earlier struggle.

Funny story

Feminist blood rose during a mid-1970s demonstration against an all-male Scottish university union, and shouts of 'Wankers! Wankers!' were heard in the elegant steets. The local paper, whether out of decorousness or deafness is not known, subsequently reported that cries of 'Pankhurst! Pankhurst!' had rallied the surging women.

On 11 August 1914 Emmeline Pankhurst declared war on Germany. The WSPU, she announced, would suspend its militant activity for the duration and, through its supporters' contribution to the war effort, would prove once and for all the value of women to the nation. Her daughter Sylvia, along with many other prominent feminists, denounced this 'capitalist war' and held to a hugely unpopular pacifist position.

As the men marched away, the process known as 'substitution' began: that is, just as chicory can in an emergency be used as a substitute for coffee, so women took the place of the Real Thing in factories, offices and transport networks throughout the country. The press loved it all, with the young women in the munitions factories proving clear favourites. A visit to a Government Training Centre inspired one (*Daily Mail*) journalist to write:

> A splendid set of girls were working in the shops, their varied coloured overalls, simply arranged hair, and bright, fresh English faces all helping to make as wonderful a warworkers' picture as can be imagined.

In munitions work, these bright, fresh English faces could soon take on a yellowish hue as a result of their owners' contact with TNT, a highly toxic substance; but the recruiting literature airily assured readers that 'the yellow colouring which appears on the skin in no way affects the health, and will disappear when the work in this department is given up for a week or so.' Who says PR's a new trade?

The seal of respectability was given to women workers when advertisers caught on to the changing market trends. A half-page advertisement in a 1917 edition of the *Daily Mail* delivered the glad tidings that, 'Munitions workers are the latest to bear most remarkable testimony to the amazing results of "Harlene Hair Drill" in securing Hair Health and Beauty.' And women workers who 'found that the grit and grime of the munitions factories, exacting hospital work, and exposure to sudden weather changes are injurious to the skin' could, according to another advertisement, take comfort in the liberal application of Ven Yusa, the 'Oxygen Face Cream'.

QUIZ

No one has asked for your opinion on the matter but you're at war. Would you:

(a) denude your budgie, splash around with some bleach and hand the white feathers to the men who intrude most on your life?
(b) start giving private tuition in German?
(c) fulfil your lifelong ambition to become a bus driver?
(d) organise tupperware parties in a munitions factory?

Well, all we can say is – thank God you did get the vote in the end.

The truth is that, although women initially got a fairly warm welcome as 'substitute' workers for men, basic attitudes towards their role in life were largely unaffected by war-time developments. Trade unionists turned apoplectic at the thought of the 'dilutees' (another popular term) being used to undercut skilled men's wages (though it rarely seemed to strike them as a good idea to consider extending their full protection to women as a sizeable and permanent part of the work force). Employers considered it their right and duty to appoint welfare supervisors to nose not only into women's work practices but also into their domestic arrangements and behaviour in the street. Government committees, like the Health of Munitions Workers Committee quoted below, pontificated in the most bizarre terms about the issues raised by increased female employment:

> Woman labour involved a physiological and a social problem. Woman was a peculiar and particular physiological instrument, and the woman labour question raised the great problems of maternity, infant welfare, and home building.

What it all seemed to mean was that, 'Everyone knows that women are first and foremost wives and mothers, with a prime responsibility for maintaining homes fit to be castles for Englishmen. How can we make sure that the present emergency doesn't mislead them into thinking anything else?'

Throughout the war years, valiant efforts were made to remind the younger generation (despite the evidence of their own eyes) of the underlying truths about male and female roles. A children's competition run by a body with the thought-provoking title, the Baby Week Council, set some gems of essay titles. Boys were invited to send in their thoughts on 'Why I Should Kill that Fly'; while girls were asked to describe 'How I Mind the Baby'. Call us dreamers if you will, but somewhere there *must* have been a little girl who took it into her head to write an essay on, 'Why I Should Kill that Baby'.

ACTIVITY Ask your granny about her literary activities during World War I.

How did women themselves feel about the transformation of their lives forced on them by war? Well, those who had been in domestic service (of whom there were, of course, hordes) seem to have been thrilled to bits; if they couldn't exactly relish the often arduous work, then at least they took great pleasure in the comparative freedom which factory work involved as well as the cameraderie of their workmates. Some found the opportunity to develop skills – in engineering, for example; though employers did their best, through the introduction of new machinery, etc., to de-skill the tasks carried out by women. Many married women with children discovered that the slightly higher wages which women often received for war work meant that they could for once eat properly: hitherto it had been generally accepted that in times of scarcity (which for many people were not infrequent) dear old Mum would hold back.

Generally speaking, despite the constant Mother of the Race propaganda, women's expectations of life were raised a little.

Imagine the shock then when, as the end of the war approached, the press spiked all the 'brave and pretty munitionettes' crap and got on with the job of urging women back to their 'proper place', meaning paid or unpaid domestic work or the traditional women's sweated trades. 'While it would be a shame,' wrote a journalist for the *Southampton Times*, 'to turn women out of their jobs at short notice in cases where such procedure would mean absolute hardship, and, perhaps, starvation, there is no reason to feel sympathetic towards the young person who has been earning 'pin money' while the men have been fighting, nor the girls who left women's work, to which they could return without difficulty, to take the places of soldiers who have now come back.'

Much to the irritation of such pundits, women showed zero inclination to return to domestic service and their other natural spheres. In fact, for many, even temporary unemployment was preferable. But hard times loomed in the 1920s and, gradually, women workers were forced back into their old stamping grounds – domestic service and the textile and clothing industries. In the new industries where women were employed, like electrical goods and engineering, care was taken to ensure that the work wasn't made too complicated and interesting. Marriage continued to be generally regarded as the cut-off point in the life of a useful female worker; after that, it was out of the workshops and into the double sink.

For young middle-class women, job opportunities were a whole lot better, with administrative and clerical work, for example, opening up a whole new future of carbon copies and mid-morning coffees (or do we mean carbon coffees?).

ACTIVITY

Cheer.

Oh yes, in 1918 those of us who seemed old enough (over 30) got the vote; and in 1928 the rest of us did too.

Self-check question

Are you old and wise enough to know what to do with the vote?

Brigid Brophy · Elizabeth Jennings · Fay Weldon
Writers 2
Jessie Kesson b. 1916
Storm Jameson b. 1897
Charlotte Mew 1869-1928 · Poet
Fanny Burney 1752-1840 · diarist
E·M·Delafield 1890-1943
Jane Austen 1775-1817
Barbara Pym 1913-1980
P·D·James Crime writer
Agatha Christie 1891-1976
George Eliot 1819-1880
Angela Thirkell 1890-1961
Sylvia Townsend Warner 1893-1978
Doris Lessing b. 1919
Ethel Mannin b. 1900
Dorothy Richardson 1873-1957
May Sinclair 1863-1942
Sybille Bedford b. 1911
Maureen Duffy
Enid Bagnold b. 1889
Molly Keane b. 1904
Harriet Martineau 1802-1876
Rose Macaulay 1881-1958
Winifred Holtby 1898-1935
Vera Brittain 1896-1970
Ruth Rendell
Geraldine Jewsbury · Margaret Drabble · A.S. Byatt · Anna Wickham
Katherine Whitehorn · Sue MacGregor · Margaret Howard

MODULE 14

A Room of One's Own: Virginia Woolf

Do you remember seeing this feature in the *Observer*?
Yes? Cut down on the booze, we implore you.
No? Well, read it now.

A Room of One's Own: Virginia Woolf

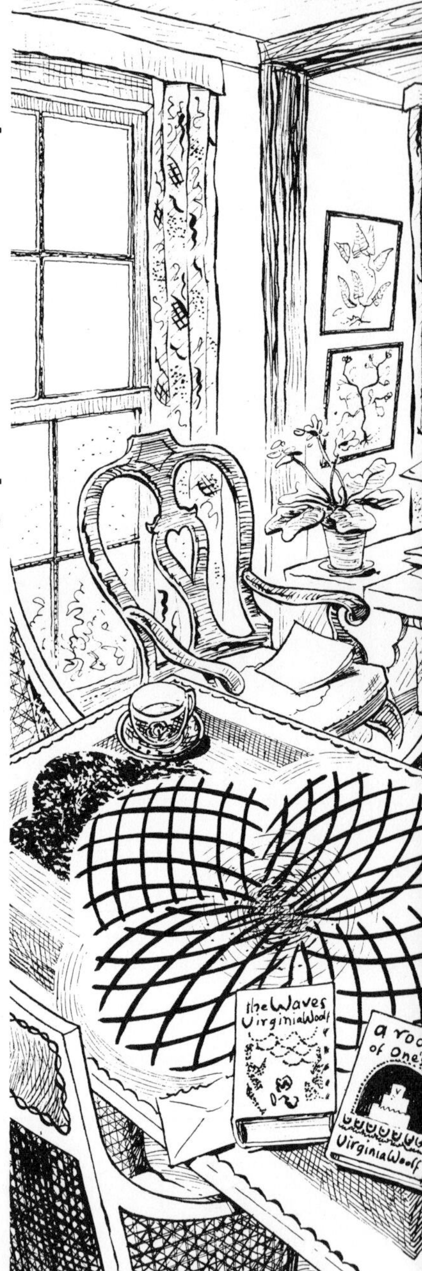

'Five hundred a year each of us and rooms of our own . . .'

With this demand for the basic essentials a woman must have if she is to write fiction, novelist, critic and essayist Virginia Woolf concluded a lecture given to Girton College undergraduates in 1928. When I visited her on a mellow late October day in 1935, she re-stated: 'Why should all the luxury of life be lavished on the Julians and Francises of the world and not on those starved but valiant young women? I told them to drink wine and have a room of their own . . . but' – with an apologetic smile – 'all the wine is drunk and my room has been demolished.'

Actually, her room (a garden 'writing lodge') was being re-erected in her orchard to give a better view across the water-meadows to Mount Caburn and the far Downs, and Mrs Woolf was offering tea and cakes from bold Wedgwood cups and plates designed by her sister, the painter Vanessa Bell.

I had come to visit Mrs Woolf at Monk's House, the writer's country home which she shares with her husband Leonard, journalist and co-founder with her of the Hogarth Press. It's a long, low, weatherboard house in the tiny East Sussex village of Rodmell; its windows look down on to a street which is little more than a dwindling cart track. The gardens (her husband's creation), orchard, meadow, pools and statuary wrap the house round on three sides. Stepping over Sally, a cocker Spaniel, and negotiating piled baskets of autumn fruits, one is decanted into a large, low room studded with colour. Late dahlias blaze outside the windows; inside too – on a country-made commode, painted in typically uninhibited style by Duncan Grant, a close friend (Lytton Strachey, another close friend, is depicted in pursuit of youthful satyrs).

Mrs Woolf removes a record from the gramophone (also by Grant; youths pursued by Mr Strachey *as* a satyr); the music is from 'The Wreckers', an opera by Dame Ethel Smythe. 'Game old cock, Ethel,' says Mrs Woolf, nodding towards a photograph of the

redoubtable composer (a close friend) propped upon the mantelpiece. 'Though I suppose you'd better not print that.' Alongside Dame Ethel are photographs of close friends T. S. Eliot, E. M. Forster, Maynard Keynes, Roger Fry, Katherine Mansfield and Lady Ottoline Morrell, picnicking in fancy-dress. (The tiled fireplace is by Vanessa Bell: fruit, flowers and eunuchs.)

The room, with its painted furniture and gay fabrics, simply shouts out 'Omega!'. Products of Roger Fry's famous art and design workshops are everywhere; naturally enough, for the artists most closely involved in this venture – Mrs Bell, Duncan Grant and Fry himself – were (and are) central figures in the group of writers, artists and intellectuals that came to be known as 'Bloomsbury'.

'Bloomsbury!' laughs Mrs Woolf. 'Mrs Nicolson' – the splendid V. Sackville-West, poet, novelist, gardener and model for the hero/heroine of one of Mrs Woolf's most successful books, *Orlando* – 'always called it "Gloomsbury" – but we had *great* fun.'

Virginia Woolf was born into an upper-middle-class literary family. Her mother, Julia Duckworth, was a famous beauty; her father, Sir Leslie Stephen, edited the 63-volume Dictionary of National Biography. On his death, the four Stephen children moved to an unfashionable address in Gordon Square, Bloomsbury, living 'communally' with friends and their cook. Advanced ideas, shocking for their time, and possibly for ours too. But this was the kernel from which the Bloomsbury Group sprang, and Virginia Stephen lived amongst them until her marriage in 1912. Wryly, she remembers taking cookery lessons as a young wife and distinguishing herself by baking her wedding ring into a suet pudding.

After moving to Hogarth House, Richmond, the Woolfs decided to buy a printing-press. Mrs Woolf was already working hard as a freelance reviewer, and in 1917 they bought a small hand-press – knowing nothing of printing, but learning as they went from a book. Publication Number 1 of the Hogarth Press was *Two Stories* – one each by Leonard and Virginia. They printed 150 copies, and followed them with Katherine Mansfield's *Prelude* and *Poems* by T. S. Eliot. Leonard printed; they both set type. '*And* bound books, pasted labels, tied parcels,' points out Mrs Woolf. 'One's fingers *ached* so. . . .'

The shelves near the fireplace contain Hogarth publications, including Mrs Woolf's novels and criticism. The success of the Hogarth Press ended many years of austere living; though one feels this period bred a frugality which has never quite left them. But Mrs Woolf sweeps her arm, saying, 'The fruits of my "making-up"! A Frigidaire here, a gramophone there . . . a Heal bed. We buy a motor-car, demolish an earth-closet – instal a WC!' One senses a certain child-like delight in her hard-earned affluence.

Mrs Woolf rolls herself another cigarette. A great case of kumquat and pineapple lolls near a Bell Conversation Piece ('Paper Games at Charleston'). More fruits of her 'making-up'? 'Not exactly. Mrs Nicolson had them sent over from Sissinghurst. I had a cold. Vita never does things by halves.'

I move to an armchair, removing a copy of *Life As We Have Known It* (Co-operative Working Women), several Lewes library books and a volume of Mrs Thrale, only to find, as I lean back, a large protuberance wedged against my vertebrae. Mrs Woolf is delighted. 'My favourite wood!', she cries. 'Bowls are our passion this year – we have a small eccentric green'. (Their lawn.)

Books and papers fill the house. Pictures, too. Roger Fry's 'Virginia rolling her own at Cassis' hangs over the mantel; to its left, Carrington's sketch, 'Lytton, as Pan, at croquet'. The large oil on the right-hand wall is Mrs Bell's 'Painters painting each other', and a small gesso panel by Roger Fry (out of picture) shows Mrs Woolf pruning an hibiscus. She cheerfully admits relying on her sister for advice over furnishing and decoration but on one aesthetic preference they disagree – Mrs Woolf's fondness for green paint. Mrs Woolf insists she is the constant butt of her family's scorn on this issue; however, the room is painted *eau de nil*.

The Omega dining table and chairs (with Mrs Woolf's monogram) are by Bell and

Grant; the folding screen by the door is Mrs Bell's – behind which, Mrs Woolf confesses, she is apt to lurk when not in sociable mood. In fact, she had planned to retreat behind it for the duration of our photo session; generally disliking photographs, Mrs Woolf only agreed to this one with reluctance.

The forescreen, a design of Duncan Grant's, was worked in needlepoint by the artist's mother; it shows a small faun lifting a dancer (J. M. Keynes and his wife, Lydia Lopokova?). Several chair covers (Bell and Grant) were worked on by Mrs Woolf herself. They are *trompe d'oeil* representations of the sort of things one would least like to find oneself sitting upon.

A painted log box (Grant: a battleship, guns garlanded, naked men swimming) is a reminder of Gordon Square days. Her brother, Adrian Stephen, with some Cambridge friends (including Duncan Grant), staged an elaborate practical joke – the notorious 'Dreadnought Hoax'. Purporting to represent the Foreign Office, they telegraphed the Commander-in-Chief of the Fleet, warning him to expect a state visit from the 'Emperor of Abyssinia', who wished to inspect HMS Dreadnought, the Navy's newest warship. Disguised by greasepaint, false beards and exotic robes, Stephen and his friends were piped aboard ship, inspected a guard of honour, had the vessel's secrets revealed to them, and declined a 21-gun salute before being escorted back to their train at Weymouth. One of the 'Abyssinians' was Virginia Stephen. The story was leaked to the press, and the Navy, furious, tried to exact revenge by kidnapping Grant for a caning. They were defeated, however, by his courage and pacifism.

'It began as a joke,' Mrs Woolf recollects. 'And a good joke it was, but it left me with a sense of the brutality and silliness of men. Those little swords . . . those pompous swags of lace . . . it disgusted me.'

Currently, Mrs Woolf is working on a new novel (*The Years*) and has been asked to write a biography of the late Roger Fry. But I left her preparing to drive back to London and her home in Tavistock Square.

'If that's where you'd called on me, you'd have come across me crouched over a gas fire, writing board on my knee, shut away behind the book boxes of our stockroom. Now, that wouldn't have made much of a picture, would it?'

MODULE 15

The Country Diary of an Overworked Landgirl

Remember all that stuff about women rallying to the flag during the First World War? Crowding into munitions factories, queuing outside any organisation likely to give them a uniform? Working like hell in horrible conditions and then losing their jobs at the end of it?

Well, the Second World War was just like that too.

As with the first time around, however, life in war-time was something of an eye- and mind-opener for many women. The Women's Land Army, for example, gave a good many the chance to experience the thrill of digging for victory.

Join us now down on the farm ...

THE COUNTRY DIARY OF AN OVERWORKED LAND GIRL
BACKS TO THE LAND
SEPTEMBER 1939
3 War declared! Decided to do my bit & JOIN UP! Love animals - (canary - tortoise) so chose LAND ARMY! Mam asked me when was I moving out?
4 SIREN WENT! Nothing happened. Was I rash? I keep thinking about the WRNS - they get Black Silk Stockings
POST OFFICE
S
I feel dead glamorous... like Katherine Hepburn..
where's t' circus, then?
NOVEMBER 1939
10 Just finished 4 week's basic training! Ready for anything, now! Going to DAIRY FARM! Wage goes up from 10/- to 22/6 pw. Sang Land Army Song.
in transit
BUCKET CARRYING PRACTICE
TARGET- 4 AN HOUR
13 FIRST BILLET! It used to be a CHICKEN SHED & I can see why. I'm in Kent, DOWN SOUTH! (Most LA lasses are from up North or London. (VERY sophisticated - but v. nice.) Tried cig. Sick.
14 Milking. Ever so tired. Up at 5am, in SNOW! - All going on about BRASS MONKEYS, but it was bad enough just finding the COWS what with the BLACKOUT! Got a cold, so can't smell a thing. Dottie (from London) says I'm in for a nasty shock, & Marlene (from Liverpool) said she'd never touch another DROP, knowing where it CAME from...
JANUARY 1940
1 Did 10 cows. War still on.
8 M. poorly. Did 15 cows. FOOD rationing! Hoarded Mars Bar.
9 D. poorly. Did 30 cows. Ate Mars Bar.
22 First lambs born! FED one with bottle. Cried. Marlene said she'd prefer it with mint sauce & peas. Horrible Farmer Pellet said she'd got the right idea
ee... it's that lovely...
gluk
guk
APRIL 1940
1 Stone-picking. Dot told me Mrs. Pellet was doing Roast Chicken AND trifle for dinner! Ever so excited! Had Mock Tripe & Suet Pudding, again. April Fooled.
3 Homesick for Mam.
5 Letter! MAM let my ROOM! Homesickness cured.
30 Sprayed fruit trees. The men won't do it, now we're here. FAINT from lack of food. Forced to escape after dark, walk 3 miles & rendezvous with mobile CHIPPY! You meet a lot of Land Girls there...
Fish Chips

MAY 1940

3 Lovely weather! On double summer-time, but nobody told the **COWS** - They're still frisky, when we're exhausted!
19 **ON STRIKE!!** — milked cows. (They don't half fill up quick). Mr. Pellet said we **EAT** too much, & docked our **PAY!!** How much do turnips **COST??** Sent wire to **WLA**, informing them of unilateral action.
23 Success! Transferring to new billet at **MOTTLEY TOWERS!** Sounds dead posh. Did milking. Mr. P. is getting **12** Italian prisoners instead of **US** to do the work. Poor things! Mrs. P's food probably violates the Geneva Convention.
24 New billet. Converted chicken shed.

Thank God they didn't give us a packed lunch.

AUGUST 1940

10 Sheared a sheep. Ever so greasy.
13 The Battle of **BRITAIN** is on!! It started right in the middle of sheep-dipping, so if we're not off catching sheep or looking for parachutists, we're taking cover in trenches, watching
16 Collective decision taken with Lady Mottley to supply poor nude sheep with **TIN HATS**

Remember, girls - one swift blow with your dibber & he's a dead man!!

24 Rations cut. Lady M. rumoured to be experimenting with **LUPIN JAM!!**

DECEMBER 1940

7 London Blitz v. bad. Dot ever so worried. about family — Kids **HAD** been evacuated, but missed chippys & couldn't stand the quiet. (Neither could I at first, but this was War Work.) They went back.
22 Learning to plough! Not v. good yet, but horses know what they're doing. Dot's family is living in a **TUBE** Station! It's got it's own magazine!
25 **CHRISTMAS DAY!** Dug sheep out of snowdrift. Grand Staff Dinner! Pud! Pheasants! Lady M. carved. Had to look out for gritty bits in bird. Turned out to be **SHOT** that killed poor thing. Had seconds.

MAY 1941

8 Learning to drive tractor. Cheese ration cut! Lady M. suggests we all go **VEGETARIAN!** (You sign a form saying you are, with witnesses. Lady **M's** got the doctor & the Vicar in her pocket, so we all did.) We all get more cheese, & fruit bars, dried bananas, & **NUTS!!** It makes sense, what with all the secret **PIG** clubs going on (the wardens & the bobbies have both got one..) & Lady **M.** going round shooting things.

GENTS
Can we give them Spam?
Snork

AUGUST 1941

...A song & a smile making life worth while
AS WE GO ALONG
SING

12 Harvest time again. Gangs of women are coming down from Up North to **THRESH**. We are surrounded by 100's of Gracie Fieldses! What little makeup **WAS** available in the shops has now gone for the **DURATION!**
Towed Binder & serviced tractor.

JANUARY 1942

1 Laying hedges. War still on. **1,000**'s of **GI**'s arriving, now America's come in.
16 Marlene met one! He had a book telling GI's about the British. It said **B****Y** was our **WORST** swear word! Ha, **HA!**
18 Fetching roots from clamp. **I** met one. He gave me some chewing gum. (They all do.) But before I'd chance to practice being Ginger Rogers, I **SWALLOWED** it! Now he knows how **BAD** the **FOOD** situation is!
30 Muckspreading with Marlene. Lady M. wrote (in Parish Mag) 'Over Paid, Over Sexed & Over Here'. The Vicar thought it wouldn't help the war effort, & **VETOED** it. **ANOTHER** Italian POW escaped from Farmer Pellet's today, & asked for asylum at the vicarage.

JUNE 1942
5 Serviced Combine Harvester. Now saving DOG ENDS & rolling own CIGS!
Dot won an ONION in the Goat & Riddle RAFFLE! She only missed the banana by a whisker.
16 Potato Picking. Tonight, all had good wash from a tooth mug, then combined Bathwater allowances for lovely deep(ish) soak. Marlene says SHE fills it up anyway. Quite shocked. Soap on ration.
RATTLE
1000 WAYS WITH AN ONION
JULY 1943
9 Fox after hens, & DIVEBOMBER after Lady M!! as she pruned her figs!! She WAS wild. Zigzagged down the lawns to the Ack-Ack Unit in the Ornamental Wood, and brought down a HEINKEL! Then rounded the CREW up at swordpoint!!
BLATTA BLATTA BLATT!
15 Dot got a BOX of Lucky Strikes! Saw 'Now, Voyager' - practised lighting cigs 2 at a time. It's not really the SAME with roll-ups. Choked.
AUGUST 1944
10 Fruit Picking. Saw 'Casablanca' for 4th. time. Ingrid Bergman must have been MAD! Marlene's found her niche in life. Ratcatching! She loves it — her jar of arsenic & her spoon - she's going in for a certificate.
if god had intended you to wear silk stockings, he'd have tattooed seams on you...
13 Cider making, hooray! Dot says her MA was in a fish queue the other day, when the siren went. Nobody moved. 1st Flying Bomb today. ALL we need.
JANUARY 1945
6 Ploughed terrace lawn. Gumboots (ordered in 1942) arrived. Wrong size. Our 4 years service armlets are a year old. I don't suppose they thought they'd need them for THAT long..
Ragout of squirrel tonight...
Would a Victory roll hairdo suit me..?
17 Ploughed grass verges. Talked about peacetime. I'd like a garage. Dot wants to run a Market Garden, & Marlene really likes ratcatching. Says they remind her of all the RATS who ran out on her! M. says Hitler's going to cop it. She saw it in the tea leaves. I said I thought they were supposed to be HIS, but she said you were allowed a bit of leeway in wartime.
MAY 1945
7 Germany surrenders! Marlene local Ratcatcher!
8 VE DAY! Gave cows extra cake, put red white & blue crêpe paper on them & cowman. Lady M. got all gooseberry champagne that hadn't exploded from cellar! Very giddy!
At night, climbed on to Downs. Beacon fires lit all along - searchlights waving far off.. town lights twinkling for first time in 6 years. We all had a bit of a cry...

● Marlene Fazackerly built up a successful pest control business, later becoming a leading campaigner for organic management and conservation of the countryside.

● Doreen Henriques was employed by Lady Mottley as farm manager, inheriting the property on her employer's death.

● Doris Pendleberry eventually married Stan Ragget, mechanic at Bott's forge and petrol pump. She is now Chair of the biggest plant hire firm on the south coast.

Politicians Activists & Reformers
Greenham
Common Women
Cecily Hamilton · Emily Faithful · Margaret Llewelyn Davies
Marie Stopes · Lydia Becker · Ray Strachey · Julia Neuberger ·
Beatrice Webb · The Sutton Female Chartists
May Hobbs · Organizer, Night Cleaners' Union
Margaret Bondfield 1873 - 1953 · 1st woman cabinet minister
Dr. Edith Summerskill 1901 - 1980 MP
Barbara Castle b. 1911 · Labour minister Euro-MP
Josephine Butler · 1828 - 1906 · Campaigned against 'Anti-Vice' Laws
Helena Wright Pioneer of Birth Control Movement
Dr. Una Kroll · Deaconess b. 1925 · Campaigner for women's rights in C of E
Dora Russell · Feminist · Pacifist · Socialist b. 1894 d. 1986
Helene Hayman b. 1949 Labour MP
Ellen Wilkinson 1891 - 1947 MP
'Red' Led Jarrow march, 1936
Emmeline Pankhurst 1857 - 1928
Suffrage Leaders
Sylvia Pankhurst 1882 - 1960 Pacifist
Christabel Pankhurst 1880 - 1958
Jennie Lee (Baroness) Supporter of Open University · Arts Minister
Constance Lytton 1869 - Hunger Strikers
Annie & Jessie Kenney · Militant Suffragettes 1879 - 1953
Frances Power Cobbe 1822 - 1904 Educationalist · Feminist ·
Winifred Ewing b. 1929 · Scottish Nationalist MP
Audrey Wise b. 1935 · Trade Unionist, MP
Elizabeth Fry · 1780 - 1845 Quaker, Prison reformer
Diane Abbot · Trade Unionist & Prospective Labour Candidate
Dame Janet Vaughan b. 1899 · FRS · Doctor, academic, feminist
Annie Besant 1847 - 1933 Radical & Theosophist
Nancy, Lady Astor 1879 - 1964 1st Woman MP
Catherine Bramwell - Booth b. 1883 · General, Salvation Army

Less than 20 years after her death, 'Battling Bessie' Braddock, Labour politician, has been virtually forgotten. Shame on us all! Having made a lot of rude and constructive noise in her time, she deserves better than a polite silence.

Born Elizabeth Margaret Bamber in Liverpool, Bessie Braddock attended her first political meeting at three weeks old, her parents being stalwart – clearly, very stalwart – radicals. Her mother, Mary Bamber, became National Organiser of the National Union of Distributive and Allied Workers and was once described by Sylvia Pankhurst as 'the finest fighting platform speaker in the country'. At her funeral, 'The Red Flag' provided the parting hymn.

Bessie was a quick learner. Liverpool's streets, not short of hungry children and the unemployed, told their own story; while the reasons for social deprivation, along with the ways to combat it, were the subject of constant discussion at home. Liverpool, after all, was a prosperous port in the early 1900s – but its poverty statistics and its rates of infant mortality were amongst the highest in the country. Bessie started by helping her mother hand out leaflets, later graduating to the post of steward at Mary Bamber's political meetings.

Her first job consisted of packing seeds in a shop, 5s. for the week. Moving on via a draper's shop she ended up at the Co-op drapery and there joined a union. Young people being fond of healthy exercise in those days, on days off she used to go cycling in the country with fellow Young Socialists. To add a bit of interest to the fresh air, they would carry stickers reading, 'SOCIALISM – THE ONLY HOPE OF THE WORKERS', and apply these bright notes to trees and cows indiscriminately. 'I must have stuck thousands on cows,' Bessie reflected in later years, whether with regret or pride is not known.

A member of the Communist Party of Great Britain for some time in the early 1920s, Bessie played a part in smuggling Communist and anarchist activists in and out of Liverpool. But the really heavy stuff started in the early 1930s when she became a member of Liverpool City Council (having acquired a husband along the way – Jack Braddock, a similarly doughty fighter). One of her lifelong passions was the desire to improve housing conditions; and she waged mighty war on the Tory Council over this issue. She had never been fond of Tories but her detestation grew as the years went on, along with her vigour of expression. 'We have a Corporation rat catcher,' she remarked, darkly, to a group of Tory councillors, 'but he goes for the wrong sort.'

During the Second World War, Bessie Braddock was a full-time ambulance driver, her vehicle having been a furniture van in an earlier life. The work was dangerous: many ambulance drivers in Liverpool were killed, 15 in one day in May, 1941. But, despite a theoretical move to an inside job, Bessie drove her ambulance through each of the 68 major air raids in Liverpool.

She had first been asked to stand for Parliament (for Liverpool Exchange) in 1936 when prospective women candidates were even rarer than they are today. But war deferred the election till 1945; and, even then, three weeks were to elapse before the result was declared in order to allow time for counting the servicemen's votes. Impatient to know how she'd done – because most pundits gave her no chance of defeating the sitting Tory – Bessie made contact with the chief assistant to the owner of a Liverpool dog track, a man well known to be a genius with figures. Having briefed the party workers on exactly what information he would need, the genius came to Bessie a few hours after the poll and told her that she had won by 620 votes. In fact, he proved to be very slightly out in his calculations: when the official result was declared, Bessie proved to have won by 665 votes. At the next election her majority rose to 5,342.

Described as 'that embodiment of the militant Liverpool housewife in Parliament', Bessie didn't take long to show the stuff she was made of – no sugar but a lot of spice. In her maiden speech, she described the slums of Liverpool as 'bug-ridden, lice-ridden, rat-ridden lousy hell holes'. If there were 20 rooms in a house, she pointed out, then there would be 20 families living in that house, with up to 9 people in a family.

Bessie had a little trouble with her constituency party in the early 1950s but she dealt with that smartish and remained serenely confident about her relationship with the broad mass of her constituents:

> Certainly my black Rover 90 with the loudspeakers on the front – and a pair of miniature boxing gloves given me by Jack Dempsey, the former world heavyweight boxer, dangling inside the windscreen – is well known around the town. People are always flagging me down to ask about National Insurance or Old Age Pensions.

Having earned the somewhat awed epithet from the *Daily Express*, 'There is nothing frail about her', Bessie turned her formidable ray gun on all that offended her, within her own party as well as in the capitalist ranks. Aneurin Bevan was not exempt. Addressing a group of women on the subject of the National Health Service, Bevan was foolish enough to say that he would not be dictated to by a lot of frustrated females. Bessie Braddock did not join in the ensuing uproar; but, meeting him a few days later in his private office in the Commons, she let rip in vintage Liverpool dockers' language. Jennie Lee subsequently commented to Bessie that she had never seen Bevan so shaken; what, she asked, had Bessie said to him. Bessie refused to tell her, wishing Nye Bevan to have to repeat it himself.

Bessie Braddock never held Cabinet office (wonder why?) but fought from the back benches until 1970. She also remained deeply involved in local government in Liverpool. But was she a feminist? An interesting question. She herself once said, 'I am not a feminist – I believe I am just as good as any man in this country.' So we can put that in our pipe, sisters; it takes quite a lot of smoking.

Epilogue

Yes, we *know* that Bessie Braddock isn't the End of History. But it all gets much harder, don't you think, as it gets closer? For this reason, we're stopping here. And, after all, you know just as well as we do What Happened Next.

Self-check question

Do you?

Sources

One book in particular has inspired us throughout our roamings in history. This is: Sellar, W. C. and Yeatman, R. J. *1066 and All That*, Methuen, 1984. First published 1930.

Module 1
Pre-history

Bradley, M., *The Mists of Avalon*, Sphere, 1984.
Dames, M., *The Silbury Treasure*, Thames & Hudson, 1976.
Hawkes, J., *Early Britain*, Collins, 1946.
Morgan, E., *The Descent of Woman*, Corgi, 1974.

Module 2
The Romans in Britain

Carcopino, J., *Daily Life in Ancient Rome*, Penguin, 1962.
Tacitus, *The Annals of Imperial Rome* (trans. Grant, M.), Penguin, 1973.
The Europa Biographical Dictionary of British Women (ed. Crawford *et al.*), Europa Publications, 1983.
Translations of Bath curses from: Hassall, M.W.C. and Tomlin, R.S.O., 'Roman Britain (Inscriptions)' sections, *Britannia*, vol. XII (1981) and vol. XIII (1982).

Module 3
Not the Knights of the Round Table

Bradley, M., *The Mists of Avalon*, Sphere, 1984.
The Europa Biographical Dictionary of British Women (ed. Crawford *et al.*), Europa Publications, 1983.
The Works of Sir Thomas Mallory (ed. Vinaver, E.), Oxford University Press, 1964.

Module 4
The Bio Tapestry

Maclagan, E., *The Bayeux Tapestry*, King Penguin, 1943.

Module 5
The Middle Ages

Ayrton, E., *The Cookery of England*, André Deutsch, 1975.
Power, E., *Medieval People*, Pelican, 1951.
Power, E., *Medieval Women* (ed. Postan, M. M.), Cambridge University Press, 1975.
The Complete Works of Geoffrey Chaucer (ed. Robinson, F. N.), Oxford University Press, 1983.

Woman of the Age:
de Pizan, C., *The Book of the City of Ladies* (trans. Richards, E. J.), Picador, 1983.

Module 6
Which Witch?

Larner, C., *Enemies of God*, Basil Blackwell, 1983.
Thomas, K., *Religion and the Decline of Magic*, Penguin, 1973.

Module 7
The Askit Letters

Jenkins, E., *Elizabeth the Great*, Victor Gollancz, 1958.
The Europa Biographical Dictionary of British Women (ed. Crawford *et al.*), Europa Publications, 1983.

Module 8
Speaking Out

Cibber, C., *An Apology for the Life of Colley Cibber* (ed. Lowe, R. W.), 2 vols, 1887.
Fraser, A., *The Weaker Vessel*, Weidenfeld & Nicolson, 1984.
Hartnoll, P., *A Concise History of the Theatre*, Thames & Hudson, 1968.
Rowbotham, S., *Hidden from History*, Pluto Press, 1974.
Shepherd, S. (ed.), *The Women's Sharp Revenge*, Fourth Estate, 1985.
The Europa Biographical Dictionary of British Women (ed. Crawford *et al.*), Europa Publications, 1983.
The Illustrated Pepys (ed. Latham, R.), Bell & Hyman, 1978.

Woman of the Age:
Duffy, M., *The Passionate Shepherdess*, Cape, 1977.

Module 9
Enlightenment: bluestockings and best friends

Boswell, J., *Life of Doctor Johnson*, Vol. 2, J. M. Dent, 1960.
Faderman, L., *Surpassing the Love of Men*, The Women's Press, 1985.
Jones, M. G., *Hannah More*, Cambridge University Press, 1952.
Mavor, E., *The Ladies of Llangollen*, Penguin, 1973.
Scott, S. *A Description of Millenium Hall*, Virago, 1986. First published 1762.
The Europa Biographical Dictionary of British Women (ed. Crawford *et al.*), Europa Publications, 1983.

Woman of the Age:
Tomalin, C., *The Life and Death of Mary Wollstonecraft*, Pelican, 1977.
Wollstonecraft, M., *A Vindication of the Rights of Woman* (ed. Kramnick, M.), Pelican, 1975.

Module 10
More than One Nation

Altick, R. D., *Victorian People and Ideas*, J. M. Dent, 1974.
Healey, E., *Lady Unknown: A Life of Angela Burdet-Coutts*, Sidgwick & Jackson, 1978.
Hiley, M., *Victorian Working Women*, Gordon Fraser, 1979.
John, A. V., *By the Sweat of Their Brow*, Routledge & Kegan Paul, 1981.
Murray, J. (ed.), *Strong-Minded Women*, Penguin, 1984.
Owen, D., *English Philanthropy 1660–1960*, Belknap Press of Harvard University Press, 1964.
The Europa Biographical Dictionary of British Women (ed. Crawford *et al.*), Europa Publications, 1983.
Vicinus, M. (ed.), *Suffer and Be Still*, Indiana University Press, 1973.

Module 11
Victorian Lady Travellers

Alexander, Z. and Denjee, A. (eds), *Wonderful Adventures of Mrs Seacole*, Falling Wall Press, 1984.
Barr, P., *A Curious Life for a Lady*, Macmillan, Murray, 1970.
Bird, I., *A Lady's Life in the Rocky Mountains*, Virago, 1982. First published 1879.
Bird, I., *Unbeaten Tracks in Japan*, Virago, 1984. First published 1880.
Middleton, D., *Victorian Lady Travellers*, Routledge & Kegan Paul, 1965.
North, M., *A Vision of Eden*, Holt, Rinehart & Winston, 1980.
The Europa Biographical Dictionary of British Women (ed. Crawford *et al.*), Europa Publications, 1983.

Woman of the Age:
Fraser, D. (ed.) *The Christian Watt Papers*, Paul Harris Publishing, 1983.

Module 12
The Further Education Game

Murray, J. (ed.), *Strong-Minded Women*, Penguin, 1984.

Module 13
Suffragettes and All That

Braybon, G., *Women Workers in the First World War*, Croom Helm, 1981.
Pankhurst, S., *The Suffragette Movement*, Virago, 1977. First published 1931.
Raeburn, A., *Militant Suffragettes*, New English Library, 1973.
Rowbotham, S., *Hidden from History*, Pluto Press, 1974.

Module 14
A Room of One's Own

Bell, Q., *Virginia Woolf, a Biography*, Hogarth Press, 1982.
Woolf, V., *The Diaries of Virginia Woolf*, 5 vols, Penguin, 1979, 1981, 1982, 1983, 1985.

Module 15
The Country Diary of an Overworked Landgirl

Sackville-West, V., *The Women's Land Army*, Michael Joseph, 1944.

Woman of the Age:
Braddock, J. and Braddock, E., *The Braddocks*, Macdonald, 1963.
Roth, A., *Sir Harold Wilson*, Macdonald and Janes, 1977.
Toole, M., *Mrs Bessie Braddock, MP*, Robert Hale, 1957.

'All That Down There'
Stone, L., *The Family, Sex and Marriage in England 1500–1800*, Weidenfeld & Nicolson, 1977.
Weeks, J., *Sex, Politics and Society*, Longman, 1981.